Praise for *Lily Was the Valley*

It seems at times to be fiction, but fiction can't compare to the reality of the heart of a man touched by a forgotten child. Dann Robert Johnson has taken us deep as he shares the mountains and valleys of this journey towards adopting a child from a foreign country. For those wishing to also do so, this book is a must. The same goes for any who have lived the adoption experience, parent or child. But the drama of turmoil in a man's soul—as a cycle of hope becomes shattered hope followed by new hope fed by persistence and even stubbornness—will take all of us to where we are confronted about our own responses to what life has dealt us.

How different it might have been had these insights been available to me in the early days of my journey.

Kelvin Gardiner, co-author of *Pastoring the Pastor: Emails of a Journey Through Ministry*. Adopted son, 1944.

Lily Was the Valley arrested me. Dann Robert Johnson has given an invaluable window into a heart-breaking, heart-testing, heart-deepening world that many have entered but few have verbalized. My own adoption experiences of despair and hope and love were relived as Dann shared a journey that was at times gut-wrenching, at-times humorous, and always honest. This book is a glimpse into a father's struggle to walk in the mysterious strains of deepest love, not a fairytale version of a princess in a castle. Lily Was the Valley is a true behind-the-scenes story of the adoption process, a story which reveals the unexpected beauty of a child, the reluctant embrace of loss, and the dramatic depths of God's love for us."

Dr. Ken Castor, author of *Grow Down: How to Build a Jesus-centered Faith* and contributing editor for the *Jesus Centered Bible*. Adoptive father, 2002.

Dann Robert Johnson writes with incredible vulnerability and honesty as he tells of his family's struggles with adoption and cross-cultural adjustment. *Lily Was the Valley* is an excellent resource for all parents and anyone dealing with the disappointments life throws at us. Dann does not write to make himself look good, but in the process of telling this amazing journey, he has become one of my heroes.

Dr. Ron Walborn, Dean, Alliance Theological Seminary

i

Lily Was the Valley is more than a poignant story. Dann's humor, authenticity, and grace invite all of us to take this journey of grief and loss, joy and hope. Like all journeys of the heart, there are no short-cuts to the end.
Victoria Chiu, LMHC, Co-founder, Crown Counseling Center

I wondered what new insights into the complexities of adoption Dann Robert Johnson might possibly offer this seven-time adoptive mother, adoption caseworker, international orphan advocate, and avid adoption-genre reader. But *Lily Was the Valley* captivated me. The privilege of following along on this adoptive *father's* journey towards his own soul—devoted and pledged to a child he'd yet to lay eyes on—was treasure. I wept, I held out hope, and I got swept away by the saga this family endured. I saw again the incalculable value of every single child who waits.
Amanda C. Hostetler, Overseas Adoptions Caseworker, Asia

I've walked with Dann and his wife Tammy through the bumpy terrain of their adoption stories and have marveled at their tenacity, their commitment, and their willingness to make themselves vulnerable again and again. *Lily Was the Valley* doesn't go the places you expect it to go, but its twists and turns provide a canvas for an unforgettable story of love, commitment, heartbreak, and remarkable faith. Even having watched the events unfold from beginning to end, I was still riveted by the story, and often moved to laughter, tears, and fresh insights by Dann's telling of it.
Maria S., founder and COO of a baby rescue home in China

Lily Was the Valley had me all the way through, laughing and crying. Dann spoke in so many deep ways to all of our core values as an organization. It's for every adopting family, regardless of spiritual views, but it will force all of us to reflect on the broken heart of a Father who has loved every child and lost so many. And on how Jesus pursues us, does not always get us right away, but never, ever, ever gives up.
-Chris Turner, Executive Director, Connect

Lily Was the Valley

Undone by Adoption

Lily Was the Valley

Undone by Adoption

Dann Robert Johnson

FLOOR
34
BOOKS

LILY WAS THE VALLEY: UNDONE BY ADOPTION
BY DANN ROBERT JOHNSON
Published by Floor 34 Books
Rolling Meadows, IL

ISBN: 9780996315807
Copyright © 2016 Dann Robert Johnson
Cover Images by Tammy Johnson
Cover Design by HanroogMOU

For more information on this book and its author, visit
www.dannrobertjohnson.com

All Scripture quotations are taken from *The Message*. Copyright © 1993,
1994, 1995, 1996, 2000, 2001, 2002. Used by permission of NavPress
Publishing Group.

Library of Congress Cataloging-in-Publication Data

Johnson, Dann Robert

Lily Was the Valley: Undone by Adoption/Dann Robert Johnson/1st ed.

To

Jenny Lynne
Alisa Ruth
Rebekka Højberg

Loved forever.

Table of Contents

Acknowledgements

THIS BOOK OWES EVERYTHING but its writing to my wife, Tammy. The story is both of ours, but without her encouragement, belief, and constant covering for me in all tasks parental, its telling might have been delayed for years. And, kids, thank you! You fantastic people have put up with more in the last few years than I care to think about. Thank you for not disowning me, and I am now ready to field questions other than, "Are you working on your book *again*, Dad?"

Thank you to all my advance readers. Michael Denneny at IEG in New York, your graciousness was doubtless a small deal to you, but it wasn't for me. Kay Bruner, your honesty was motivational. Susan Yao Shu Juan, thank you for your invaluable Chinese perspective and proofreading of my Chinese quotes. Weldon, your precision was a true eleventh-hour blessing. For the book cover—and the learning process that got me there—I am grateful to Sung McClure, K. Wolfram, and HanroogMOU.

Thank you, Ben Cubbage, for DDQ Wild, and Chris, Jason, Mark, Clara, Benjamin, and Jamin for your outrageous encouragement, not just to walk up a mountain, but to dream. This book got finished when it did because of you guys. Kirti Gilbert, your killer quote for the expat list was bested only by your genuine affirmation of all our story meant to you personally. Maria Sell, thank you for being yourself. Your steadfastness in saying what you really thought made this book better than it could have been without you.

Jody Ingalls, thank you for everything. (Is there any more

clutter I should cut from that?)

Phil Steiner, my most faithful editor, you will forever be linked in my mind to the Oxford comma. It would be impossible (okay, okay…*nearly impossible*) to overstate the effect you have had on this book. I could go on for paragraphs about your greatness, and I seriously considered doing so just for the pleasure of getting this sent back to me with "bloviation" scrawled in the margin one last time. Thank you for reading, for sitting and talking, for re-reading, for being a sounding board, for answering my every email, and for reading some more. If this is a perfect book, it's because you are that good. If it is not, then you should have sacrificed some more of your life for me. But, for the percentage you already did sacrifice, I will remain grateful forever.

Kelvin Gardiner, there has never been a time—not during the story told in this book, nor during the saga of writing it down—when I did not know your unfailing support. You were this book's first fan before I'd even started, and you remain its biggest one. You repeatedly cheered me on just when I needed it most, and *Lily Was the Valley* owes much to your unconditional love for me.

Finally, thank you to my Lord, Savior, Brother, and Friend, Jesus Christ. Those aren't empty words, which those who've read the story already know.

And one more…Thank you to all these purchasers of a *Lily Was the Valley* pre-sale reward level: Nathan Dean, Norma and Barry Hinds, Jody and David Ingalls, Larry and Joyce Johnson, Chris and Tammy Moore, Bob and Marge Rightnour, Sandy Robertson, Jarri Servadio, Nettie J. Zekveld, Carolyn and John Berggren, Charla Bolind, Pedro Cortes and Crystal Cooper Cortes, Christy and Jeff Dooley, Cristian and Kelly Nelson, Don and Patty Poorman, Brad Rightnour, Brett and Brenda Zook, John and Joy and Andrew, Christian and Isa Bossy, Patrick and Krista Hastings, Mary and James Kidd, Brent and Lisa Liberda, Eric and Flora Lui, Linda South, Tamara York, Jim and Challise Cantleberry, Nathan

Cantleberry, Stuart and Ruth Carlson, Alec and Brenda Chien, Casey and Jennifer Davis, Shanna Dawson, Harold Emsheimer, Kathy Gross, Niel and Mara Haggmark, Brad and Abby Houdashelt, Chantelle Howell, Bryan and Amy Johnson, Diane Lee Johnson, Carol Kennedy, Patricia and Rick Love, Becky McClelland, Sharon Getter Mitchell, Darlene Moitoso, Jim and Lisa Morris, Katrina Nisly, Jacqueline Olive, Clara Pang, Chaney Poston, Mark and Cori Salchert, Elizabeth Secora, Elissa Seid, Todd Speary, Elianne Sussenbach, John and Susannah Wisley, Christine Zidek, Stephen and Gail, Daniel and Amanda Bray, Jennifer and Mark Cameron, Sheila Carr, Penny Cheung, Krysta Colby, Brian and Michelle Davis, Daniel and Stephanie Dias, Robb and Heather Fried, Reese and Jennifer Graves, Julia Hageman, Martha Harris, Claudia and Jonathan Juzi, Kerrie Kaufmann, Sheva and Terry Leon, Vanessa K. Magnus, Ashley Mason, Bob and Molly Midgette, Christopher and Erin Moore, Dan Morse, Dave and Kami Oldenkamp, Jeff and Sarah Owens, Joel Pan, Tim and Sarah Platt, Clara and Mark Szto, Jason and Natasha Tompkins, Jonathan and Katie Trevino, Anne Millikin.

Introduction

WE ARE, ALMOST WITHOUT fail, deeply moved by the births of our children. That glimpse of a firstborn's head peeking into the world for the first time is enough to overwhelm just about anybody with the awe of birth. The breath catches and the mind careers…Is this really happening? The smiles can't be stopped. Everyone is crying.

Miracle.

People are less moved by the birth of a friend's child, and not at all by the births of most children. Birth is seldom connected with miracle by anyone but those close to one. For it occurs with such saturating frequency as to render it effectively commonplace.

Adoption, too, has become common, though episodes of adoptive parents meeting their child for the first time look quite different from births. Mom and Dad still are nervous. They are joining hands, waiting for that first glimpse. There she is. She's dressed. Wearing shoes someone else put on her that morning. She returns their gaze. Is she aware of who they are? It's hard to tell.

Here, too, though, Mom and Dad can't stop smiling. Here, too, there is crying.

Also miracle.

To those on the outside, an adoption match seems the furthest thing from miraculous. What other result could a family expect after paying an agency to arrange that match? It's almost as sure as what I expect once my wife's belly begins to resemble a watermelon.

We experienced both—birth and adoption—as miracles because we were on the inside.

You have a son.

You have a daughter.

Here, hold him.

Here, we have three pictures of her.

Wow! Can you believe how teeny his feet are?

Can you believe she's ours? Look at that adorable ear.

But the empirical phenomena conspiring to elbow miracle from the picture are everywhere. They would commend a more natural view. Seek to nudge out allowance for any breaches in the natural order.

Did you have relations with this woman?

Yes, of course I did.

Did you pay fees and fill out forms for your adoption agency?

Guilty as charged. A multiple offender.

On both counts.

But just as the miracle of birth is not reducible to its own biological processes, no adoptive match is the pairing of two file folders alone. Yes, it is that—the expected and natural result—but it is far more. On our match day, we became connected to Lily by that invisible, mythical thread of fabled Chinese red, never to be broken.[1]

Quite meaningful for us as insiders.

For the outsider it's a story among millions, a yawn, and the only benefits to be gleaned from infinite tales of forms, documentation, phone calls, and photocopies would be neuroleptic. For the outsider, not even struggle, neglect, trauma, or death would be sufficiently sensational a draw, though *Lily Was the Valley* has all of those.

No, a memoir (at least the memoir of any non-celebrity) must have more. If it's going to be worth reading, it must go places that prove, even in their specificity, universal. It must go beyond, or beneath, what is visible.

Our adoption narrative will not take the turns you may expect —indeed it did not take the turns anyone expected—but those turns form only the framework for story.

Yes, Lily was our valley.

The real story is the invisible story.

Lily Was the Valley

Undone by Adoption

Prologue

I HAD THOUGHT WE would be the ones to profoundly change her life. An orphan? Coming to belong in a family? Blessing itself.

But no.

Pain—even death—lay waiting. For all of us.

The night before I would finally meet Lily, I wrote her a letter.

> My Dearest Lily,
>
> I have done little else the past twelve hours other than think of you. The morning will find me on my way to see you. You, of course, won't recognize me, as we've never seen each other. In fact, you may be in for a bit of a rude awakening as your noodles and your chopsticks and your *baozi* and whatever else your favorites are and your aunties and your friends all soon disappear! But don't worry, there will be many, many wonderful things, too.
>
> A family.
>
> I will love you for as long as I live, Lily. I know, I don't under-stand it myself. Thank you for inspiring me. It's my privilege to love you, although a bit overwhelming and scary sometimes to feel so much when I can't explain it. I know there are many more chapters of understanding to come.
>
> I will see you in the morning…

At some points in every adoption journey, all is hope and anticipation and joy.

Part I

Difficulty

With a Capital D

NO ONE TOLD US about the screaming.

In the early stages, still filling out paperwork, I thought the hard part would be simply accomplishing this thing called adoption. But paperwork and long waits would prove to be nothing to the war our daughter brought into the house.

I had taken no courses and done little reading. My realm had been the paperwork, and I'd plowed through it with due diligence and left the nurture stuff to my wife. I judged myself prepared. This was our fourth kid; I was not in the "clueless new parent" category. I was hardly a candidate for a class on how to be a dad.

But I was mistaken.

Nothing debilitates quite like being clueless about your own cluelessness. Somehow I missed the memo that adoption difficulties often stretch for years beyond finalization. Somehow I hadn't learned that negligible touch and scant nurture in the first year of life can alter the human brain indefinitely. I had never heard the words *sensory, processing,* and *disorder* together in one sentence. I'd had no reason to think about neurotransmitters or synapses since college biology. I had never considered that the cerebral health of our new little family member might be something I should concern myself with. I had not one clue about significant differences between rearing adopted versus biological children.

Even once those differences had walloped me over the head, I was still ignorant about what to do about them. Doors onto life-giving adoptive theory were only opened to us years later when we got involved in our second adoption. Meanwhile, our first three months of adoptive life were difficult beyond expectation—exponentially so. Those three months got seared into memory. Having been a dad three times already counted for almost nothing.

Our difficulties with paperwork and waiting would fade to nostalgia.

The screams were bloodcurdling.

Every night before the storm I would sit in the rocking chair and hold her, reading books and singing. Once the drama began, I would cuddle her close, hoping to exhaust her. The screaming and sweating and pushing and fighting were hard to endure if listening from the rest of the house, let alone close up, but I held on. I was loving and patient most of the time, but at others just as exasperated and exhausted as she.

Out-stubborn me, will you, little girl? I don't think so.

I was doing what came naturally in the course of desperation. I knew nothing about holding time as method; we were surviving. My daughter needed sleep, and this helped her get there. She slept better exhausted. Getting her there quickly became preferable to four hours of fidgeting and fussing only to have to end up enduring the scream session anyway. Nights when she dropped off immediately for an hour's doze were the worst. It only freshened her for true death matches.

Three hours, every night. I can hear the screams still. They could start at seven and finish at ten, or start at nine and finish at midnight. Occasionally it seemed wiser to keep her up later to tire her. In reality it only meant starting at eleven and finishing at two, so we tried it seldom. There were no days off: seven nights each week, three hours each night, like clockwork.

We didn't love her.

Not always, anyway. Not by a long shot. It tore my wife apart. Tammy had been so in love during the waiting process, and she reeled with guilt over those good feelings being supplanted by frustration, irritation, and anger. Once in a while we soared to apathy, but more often we went the other way. Emotions leaked out that just a few months earlier Tammy would have thought herself incapable of feeling: loathing, disgust, dislike. I had them, too, just didn't struggle with the guilt. It likely didn't help matters when I invented silly, cynical lyrics to the "Hush, Little Baby" song I sang her every night. Papa's going to buy you everything you never wanted, kid. Unfortunately I sang it one night while my other kids were listening in, and they never quit asking for "that totally hilarious other version" afterwards.

Our naiveté kept us from knowing that what we were going through was far from uncommon, so there was little to comfort us. We pitied ourselves.

Had adopting been a terrible mistake? We found ourselves verbalizing such things, only to be even more horrified to think the kids had overheard them.

Her cry was like no cry any of them had ever made. For they, touched and cuddled and cooed over since birth, subconsciously possessed deep knowledge about where they were, who they were, and whose they were. The knowledge was part of them, as real as their looks or their personalities. They were home. They were themselves. They were ours.

Our fourth child's brain had instead been overloaded as an infant with a struggle for survival. Her psyche had no room for those other questions, or their answers. She was missing cerebral and neurological capacity that we had assumed were a given. They aren't. Her brain had not been given the environment for normal postnatal development.

Instead of the security and safety our other children had known, this baby had known abandonment and neglect. She knew that closing her eyes in one world could mean waking up in a frightening new one. That fear brought on desperate struggle. Sleep, along with a great deal else, must be fought with every fiber of one's being.

A Birthday Party

Two years later

THE HOUSE SMELLS LIKE chocolate. The cupcakes are frosted.

Tammy is headed outside to get a quick photo shoot of our birthday girl in an unspoiled princess dress. Little party friends will soon be arriving.

"Honey, I'll call before we come back up. Can you have everyone ready to sing?"

"Be happy to, dear."

And bye-bye, Princess, you precocious little button of a cutie-pie, you. Is it possible this is already our second birthday party for you? You turn three today...how far you've come.

Indeed, our entire family has come a long way since completing the adoption and bringing our daughter home almost two years ago.

It has been a longer and more winding road than anyone came close to warning us it might be. More difficult than we could have imagined. But now this brown-eyed spitfire is more precious to us than, at many points along the way, we could have ever imagined either.

Her adoptive beginnings have been an open storybook since she came to us. I recount the details for her in bedtime tales that she loves hearing, especially the part when we come for her. The sad parts, where a baby lies in her crib with no one to love her, I make up as best I can. I know that somewhere a woman gave birth to her. I do not know if those first parents named her or how they loved her, nor am I ever likely to. Nobody knows all of the reasons

8

that baby came to be in that crib. Now three years old, she hasn't asked. We know some questions are only a matter of time: Why am I the only one in our family with black hair? Why doesn't anyone else have brown eyes? If Elijah was in your belly, and I wasn't, then… But so far she hasn't asked.

The party has a theme.

The theme is princess. Was it ever going to be anything else?

Maybe the next year a four-year-old's universe would revolve around Pippi Longstocking, and that near antithesis to princess would lend her thematic party presence to everything from the cake to a horse that guests could lift overhead to the laughably dubbed Swedish movie from the sixties. But not this year. This year is princess—all princess. After all, dress-up and music and dancing are the Princess's daily regimen.

The Princess is above all devoted to Belle. Her love for that Beauty eclipses that for any other. Is it subconscious identification with Belle's hair and eye color? Or maybe it's Belle's beautiful voice. Perhaps it is the dance Belle shares with the Beast. The Princess loves all those things. In fact, only one love surpasses the love that she has for dancing, music, and Belle:

Chocolate. The party was always going to be princess, and the cupcakes were always going to be chocolate.

I go to the window, looking for the photo shoot now taking place a dozen floors below.

There. A flash of twirling pink in the green clover. The dress is just a generic frilly one. The official character dresses from when her big sister was this age are long gone. None would have properly fit this petite pixie from southern China anyway, and besides, none of them could have heightened the glee sparked by this delicious pink one.

Arms swooping, dress swirling, hair flying…Mommy captures every pose. The contrast between the bald, unresponsive one-year-old in the Guangzhou White Swan Hotel and this silly, vibrant, huggable imp in the pink dress is miraculous. The transformations that have turned that screaming one-year-old in my tired arms to this jumping three-year-old in the flowers and clover are almost more than I can take in. Not without laughing in amazement.

There are no indications that adoption, even now, has yet to deal us its worst.

Yet getting to this point has not been easy for any of us.

She Married a Complete Pain Noob

不怕慢，就怕站

Be not afraid of growing slowly,
be afraid only of standing still.

Chinese Proverb

"Who do you want, her or the other three?" had an obvious answer:

I'll take the three. They're a piece of cake.

Just prior to adoption, bedtime had been an easy case of divide and conquer. Six years separated our oldest from our youngest, the girl separated the boys, and both parents doing the job together was our preferred system. If one of us happened to be out, then the other would get stuck with the disagreeable job of doing everything alone. After adoption, putting the three to bed became the coveted prize, a task easily finished hours before the other would wind down.

You are going to go to sleep, my girl, and my strong arms will be here until you do. I am not concerned about you being hot or uncomfortable or terrified or overtired. If I put you down and leave you, you're going to scream just the same or worse anyway. Then we'll be back again in an hour doing this same thing. Let's just get it over with now, shall we?

Had we known the profound role that orphanage life had played in our daughter's brain formation, it could have helped us better understand all that was going on. But we didn't.

She was the furthest thing from normal, yet we had no idea that her needs were completely different from those of our biological three at that age. I felt an urgency to get her caught up in all the ways she was behind. We would have done far more good treating her like a newborn, but we pushed to acclimate her to the family routine.

It only exacerbated our doom.

. . . .

Tammy had grown accustomed to a certain level of clueless-ness from her husband over the years. Especially when it came to emotional empathy. Myself, well, I defaulted to couching my traits in more positive terms:

I was patient.

Had been patient all my life. And patience, as everyone knows, is a virtue.

How shocking in the early days of marriage to have had some of my virtues exposed as something less. My new bride often found herself hard-pressed to praise my particular brand of patience. She would have as soon called moss patient. Moss on a log. Sitting there. Doing nothing. Growing for years and you still can't tell whether or not it's moved. Check again, maybe it moved when the log rotted and fell to earth last winter. Nope, it's still there. Still not moving.

She dared to call my virtue *passivity*.

On the flip side, Tammy had some virtues that her new husband found to be something rather less as well. In her self-promotional dating brochure, had she such a document, she'd have listed "careful" and "proactive" under virtues. But I hadn't known her six months before I could see what really drove some of that stuff. Fear.

We were both finding marriage a wake-up call.

Not caring to be called passive, I dug in, less apt to act than ever.

Which only fed Tammy's fears.

Which only strengthened my resolve to stand firm until she learned some patience. I could not allow myself to be moved by irrational fear. That would be an affront to my manhood.

11

Tammy was wondering where the manhood was.

Thus stood our particular mixture of imperfect marital soil at the time we decided to start a family. We had always spoken of having children. Perhaps three. For sure not just one, and heavens, nothing like six. There was little reason to bring adoption into the picture. That conversation was for another era, and irrelevant in light of the top priority, procreation. To start a family, we only needed (I noted in a turn of simplicity-laced brilliance) to turn our full attention to that.

Instead, we plunged into the crucible of infertility.

Before marriage, watching Tammy be afraid of things I didn't know anyone could be afraid of bemused me. After marriage, I learned these fears were going to affect my life immensely, whether it be driving into the city, noises at night, or me wanting to go on a guys' trip. In our heated discussions about fears any rational person could see were irrational, I found my patience, well…hard to find. Tammy could fear things that hadn't begun to materialize. When I couldn't predict what I'd feel past tomorrow's dinner, she could fear the future as if the worst were a given.

She did it as soon as we decided to start a family.

"What if we can't get pregnant?"

Excuse me? We haven't even begun and we need to start worrying?

This poor lass needed a reality check. My clearly superior view of the world would be just the ticket—was *I* in inner turmoil?—and I would help her change. She would welcome a release from the havoc of her over-emotionalism, I was sure of it. Life would be better being more like me.[2]

As I had no means of actually guaranteeing anything regarding fertilization, I set about exposing the holes in her logic. My wife had asked a question. Questions require answers. Or sometimes, in cases where answers cannot be found, ridicule works nicely to cast doubt on the validity of the question itself. For none of these services would I require of her so much as a thank-you in return.

I eased in by pointing out the societal landscape. It demanded our optimism. Look around: people who want to have children have children. Nearly all of them. And so would we. Far and away the majority of people who try, succeed. Why belabor the exceptions? There were the facts of life, and there was statistical probability. Put them together, my dear, and our quest has nothing but the highest mathematical likelihood of succeeding.

To my consternation, Tammy took no solace in mathematical

comfort.

"But what if we can't get pregnant?"

Married so briefly, and already I was in over my head.

"Dear, why worry so early? We have every chance of getting pregnant, so why fear that we won't?" Again I went over how silly it was to talk of failure before we'd even begun.

"But what if? Maybe we won't get pregnant."

Tears were shed far earlier in the ordeal than I could understand. They only flowed more freely with every passing month. Dratted statistical probability failed to come through for me. A few negative test results were all the confirmation Tammy needed that her fears were justified. I stood by helplessly, conscious only that her reactions were out of all proportion to what I experienced as reality. I quit talking so much and lived in a state of mystification over the strength of her emotions. I offered no disingenuous words of encouragement. Marriage had already cured me of that "virtue."

More months went by. Our dissimilarities increased. I assumed every month would be the one. Things were going to work out. We were young, and I was patient. At least used to be. Tammy, on the other hand, grew more anxious. She knew something was wrong. She was infertile. Or I was.

I agreed that—while still insisting that a little delay was no reason to despair—it couldn't hurt to visit the doctor. When his exam exposed the fallacy in her gloomy assumptions, I kept my mouth shut. When his comments exposed my ironclad optimism as even more ignorant, I examined my nails. He said there was a litany of possible problems the initial testing was powerless to detect. Tammy's fear remained. She'd had friends who had known infertility. Her fear of facing such years of pain bordered on panic. Still I could not understand her. Or her pain.

Our months of trying and failing stretched to a year and kept going. My own journey of Bewilderment, Indefatigable Optimism, Confusion, or Just Plain Waiting estranged me more and more from all she was going through. I could not relate, and was of no consolation to her on her journey, Pain.

Here's the truth of the matter: I was not even within waving distance of understanding the losses my wife was feeling. The dreams she saw dying. I had no capacity for comprehending loss because I had never known loss. My childhood held no trauma, and my transition from loving family to independent adulthood had left me unscathed, and, if you had asked me, mature. When faced with my wife's suffering, I thought loving her meant offering her a hand up onto the higher ground of emotional stability. Sad to say, I believed her pain, at least in part, was a natural extension of things she could have changed about herself if she had wanted to. If asked which of the two of us struggled with emotional deficiency, I would have returned a knowing wink and assumed the question rhetorical.

Meanwhile, I didn't have a clue how to really love Tammy during her deep trial. Infertility is difficult, but she had the added difficulty of a husband who hardly understood that, or her. I never saw the greater roles I could have played. Pain remained inscrutable to me because I had not known pain. I couldn't understand its effects even on the person I knew and loved the best. She carried her pain alone.

In terms of everything that adoption would one day throw our way, I was woefully ill-equipped.

. . . .

Once it had been thrown my way, I ignorantly believed I could overcome my new daughter's sleeping problems with superior strength of will. As her ability to understand English improved (we ourselves spoke none of the dialect her former caregivers spoke, so our Mandarin was useless), she and I developed a system whereby I would give her something in return for her lying still. It worked pretty well, and she would nod in the dark that she wanted me to release first a hand, then an arm. We could both relax in the mo-mentary stillness of a temporary ceasefire, no sounds but the squeak of the rocking chair and its two occupants catching their breath.

Usually at some point the screaming and pushing would start back up again.

But eventually at some other point she would also go limp, like a washcloth and just as wet. Especially her head. She could sweat buckets, and I would be soaked through from holding and rocking her. More than once during those weeks, I would be at my office and suddenly notice my back and arms and neck were sore, and wonder why.

I haven't done any physical labor, no exercise. Oh no, I hope I'm not getting the flu...and then I would recall the rocking chair from the night before.

Adoption was so different from everything I thought I'd been signing up for.

Adoption's First Beginnings: Conflicted to Say the Least

忽冷忽热

Now hot, now cold.
Or, To alternate.

Chinese Saying

I ONCE LOVED A girl.

Kitty was the most mysterious girl in all of second grade. Her eyes could capture a boy's soul with a glance. She even spoke to me once.

But I do not mean that girl.

Nor do I mean the flautist in my sixth-grade band. My budding love for tall, smashing Dawn was slightly less childish, but my world barely bordered the worlds in which she would soon be starring. Jazz band, tap dancing, the cool boys. Cool boys didn't wear Huskies.

I do not mean that love.

I am not speaking, either, of my youthful love for my high school girlfriend, nor of my pretended love for the list of girls I obtusely joked about liking during the same time.

The girl is none of them.

The girl is not even my wife, though our love is real and true, spanning decades, transforming.

I am not speaking here of that love.

I loved a different girl.

It was not love at first sight, for never had I seen her. I loved her without sight.

A love skeptic, practically, taken by surprise. Blindsided.

Blindsided by love at no sight.

. . . .

Adopting had not been my idea.

My wife had been thinking about adoption since she was a teenager, and even while dating we'd discussed it a few times. Adopting sounded fine to me, and when she continued mentioning it after marriage and after we had kids—we ended up not being infertile after all—it still sounded fine. But I considered it something for the future. Someday, sure, let's adopt.

But one day Tammy pressed a little. The whole family had been discussing adoption quite often of late, and our four-year-old daughter had been regularly praying that God would make it happen. "Honey," Tammy asked, "are you seriously up for adopting? Honestly, truly? I mean, are you okay if I start researching adoption agencies that we could use?"

I looked at her. I *had* been thinking it over. I had no real objections, no reasons it absolutely had to be later rather than now, so I innocently ignited her dry tinder with two words:

"Why not?"

Within hours, pamphlets, packets, and portfolios came flying in from all over the country. The kitchen table listed dangerously.

"Oh, you meant, like, right now, did you?"

Whereas I might take days weighing the pros and cons of a pair of shoes, research for Tammy did not entail sitting around on one's brains all day.[3] Research was an action verb. She looked at me with a twinkle and shot back, "Why not?"

. . . .

"Hello?"

It's the director of adoption services from our adoption agency. She's never called me before. It's a sunny spring day, and

17

the windows and both sunroofs of our borrowed silver minivan are wide open. I have parked on the side of the road to take the call, and my wife is passing out snacks to our children—ages seven, five and one—in the back.

"Mr. Johnson, I have a little girl for you."

"Are you joking?" I hear myself ask, grinning. As if the director might reply, *You got us, Mr. Johnson. We just love prank-calling our waiting families.*

I'm embarrassed.

I swivel to face the passenger seat, cover the phone, and, still grinning, mouth one word in a silent shout: "Referral!"

Raised brows and a blank stare.

Jabbing my finger toward the phone, I mouth it again, slower. Still nothing. My wife, absolutely unhampered in any other mode of communication, is a hopeless lip reader. Yet, unaccountably, I mouth my capitulation to her as well. "Never mind!"

I go back to the call and she goes back to the snacks. I learn the little girl's special need—a cleft soft palate, no cleft lip—and the province where her orphanage is located.

With my question, "When was she born?" my wife is finally in cahoots. I catch a view of her hands flapping. We've been waiting for this a long time. The joy spreads to her feet, her arms, her whole body. She narrowly misses ejecting from the vehicle entirely.

Another question or two and I hang up.

My wife is crying. I am crying.

The kids cry, "Why are you crying?"

We explain, and they get excited too. Our crying turns to laughing: a mysterious sister-to-be has become real. Her arrival is near.

Even the one-year-old is laughing.

It was pure fun, that call.

April 15. Tax day in the United States. We took the call in Texas but had spent the previous four tax days out of country, so April 15 for us had already begun to lose some of its usual consequence. Now it was gone for good. Henceforth, April 15 would be Lily Day. The day we got the call. The day an idea—that we would add to our family via special needs adoption from the People's Republic of China, our second home—became reality. We were matched.

We got the van back on the road and drove, madly scanning for wireless so we could download the referral email. We found an open network in some parking lot and gazed wonderingly at three pictures of a girl who had not yet been named Lily when they were taken. In the next two days, we would forward translated documents and measurements to our pediatrician, await her medical opinion, and submit our official written acceptance letter. Not until then would the referral become the official match.

But grinning and crying there in our sunny van, we already knew.

It was gonna be love.

. . . .

Or was it?

I had the dubious distinction of falling in love with my wife three years after I'd married her. We'd been at a retreat where my heart came so alive and felt so raw that I wondered it didn't burn a hole through my chest and fall to the street. Every breath pressed me up against a world I'd never known existed. Feeling everything, I saw how accustomed I was to feeling next to nothing.

"Do you mean to tell me that you live like this all the time, Tammy? Like, you know exactly what you feel all the time, without having to stop and think about it?"

She laughed at me. "Yes, dear, of course. I am a woman."

I couldn't believe some people—men or women—had been walking around their whole lives like that.

But we went home, and the boil subsided. The old me returned. I just wasn't the passionate, or compassionate, type.

I'd always held my wife's compassion, on the other hand, in a bit of awe. For instance, when it came to orphans, she could sit down to look at webpages full of children waiting for families... and actually feel things. Not me. I generally had one emotion looking at pages like that: overwhelmed. There were thousands of such kids. Far too many to feel anything for them individually. Tammy would look into the eyes of a little face and be filled with compassion. I saw strangers. Kids I didn't know, far removed from me.

I couldn't imagine crying over one of them, and logic ensured I never would. For how could tears for one not highlight how all the rest were being ignored? And not just from that webpage but from

19

countless others like it? There was no way to feel compassion for one child because I knew I couldn't feel compassion for all of them. I could gaze at children with missing limbs, a cleft lip, or cerebral palsy and be sobered or grow pensive; but I never experienced heartbreak as Tammy did.

For the most part I felt nothing.

Had I seen a picture of Lily before Lily Day, I would not have taken special note of it. I would not have thought her especially beautiful. I was excited the first time I saw her picture because someone had just told us she was ours. But, like after the marriage retreat, excitement faded. I was as taken with imagining the process behind the scenes that had whittled down those endless pages to one child as I was with the child herself.

Will I be able to love this child like I love Enoch, Haddie, and Elijah?

I didn't know.

Even while our firstborn, Enoch, had grown in my wife's belly, I'd not been able to predict what I would feel at his birth. It took that first glimpse to bring the tears that I had honestly not known would come or not. And of course the births of Haddie, our daughter, and Elijah, our made-in-China boy, moved me, too.

But ahead of time? Feelings remained just out of reach. With Lily, all we had were a few pictures. Yes, we knew she was eating, drinking, growing, crawling, teething. But she did not feel real. I couldn't help but think about how—up until our match—she had been one among nameless thousands. We couldn't see her, nor would we see her until we went to sign the final papers. What would I feel up until that time? Would adoption lead to genuine feelings of love in me?

I had no idea.

I thought it just as likely I'd end up feeling nothing at all.

. . . .

Of course, the day would come when feelings about adoption were no longer ambiguous for me, as struggle would have by then personified itself in the wiry body of a screaming girl who had launched a campaign to take over our world.

20

The Boring Part

There is something more terrible than a hell of suffering—
a hell of boredom.

Victor Hugo, *Les Misérables*

THOUGH "OUR DIFFICULTIES WITH paperwork and waiting would fade to nostalgia" once the days of the screamer arrived, they were no picnic at the time we were going through them. For into the life of every prospective adopter comes a word, a word striking fear, a fear so real and so near, that unless a drop of water to wet the mouth, or a piece of hankie to wipe the brow, may be found immediately, the will to proceed just might be vanquished before one can even begin. Some speak the word only in a whisper:

Dossier.

Okay, it's not quite as sinister as all that. The dossier is the initial paperwork packet that gets sent to China (if you're adopting from there) and enrolls a family on the master list of families awaiting matches. The dossier experience must be lived in order to be appreciated, although *appreciate* is almost certainly the wrong word. The dossier is taxing in the extreme, culling data from every extrasolar corner of paternal and maternal universes alike, no era too remote, no historical connection too dim. Completing the dossier requires more stamina than brilliance, and many who would struggle to define, yea, spell *bureaucratic acuity* have run the gauntlet and passed through with flying colors. But the faint of heart would do better to give up before starting.

Many adoption memoirs before this have masterfully chronicled the chilling particulars of the clerical black hole that is the adoption dossier; the reader of this one shall be spared the terror.

I myself was ill-suited to tackling such a monstrosity, so I was fortunate to have a chipper wife by my side cheering me on, and I got moving. The agency had provided a task list so long as to be almost beyond all cognitive grasp: letters, documents, notarizations, state seals, and embassy authentications *ad nauseam*. Our mad hope was to figure everything out and be finished, working on it as full-time as we could, in two months.

"We're having a baby!" we started telling people.

"And I'm the one in labor!" said I, the one assigned most of the jobs. So clever.

Sure enough, in two months we'd summited our paperwork mountain like a couple of regular Sir Edmund Hillarys,[4] on schedule. Our first hurdle had been leapt. We raced to the nearest copy machine and wiped out a small stand of trees making the required dossier quadruplicates. Off went the originals to the agency. They would make the next shipment to China at the end of the week.

We began stage two.

The Long Wait.

No one becomes a revolutionary hero for participating in The Long Wait, but it, too, nonetheless requires fortitude. Some families are waiting as I write this sentence. Some families are waiting as you read this one. And some families had their wait stretch out to incorporate all the time between the two.[5] There are waits of months, there are waits of years, and some have waited more than ten years. Our minds had already turned to slush in our attempts at navigating this strange new universe comprised entirely of acronyms, where fingerprints expire, and behind every step lurk ten more.

Families waiting at that time for an adoptive match from China were about to see their wait times double, though none of us knew that. Months went by. No matter which part of the process we found ourselves waiting in, it all seemed long. I determined one day to distract myself from another day-sweat picturing our dossier inch across someone's desk. I made a list of all the differences I could see between expecting this baby and what it had been like to expect our other three:

Pregnancy is a very exciting time building toward one special date on the calendar: the due date. It is written in ink months ahead of time. It might be off, but it won't be by much.

Adopting has building excitement toward countless due dates. There are more due dates than items on the dossier checklist. The big ones like LID and LOA and Article 5 and TA are generally celebrated with enough ballyhoo to make the casual observer ask if the adoption home study had turned up any insanity in the family.

Pregnancy, often planned, may also come to a couple unplanned. Since the beginning of time people have procreated and borne children. It is an unstoppable force. It just happens.

Adopting is always premeditated. It is a conscious response to need or desire. It does not just happen. The dossier-savvy quip that people do not practice unprotected paperwork, and they do not experience unplanned adoptions.

Pregnancy is timed. Everyone knows basically how long it is going to take.

Adopting is not timed in the least. There are people who signed up for an adoption program with promises of a one-year wait and may have waited four. Or twelve. Others could have planned for four and waited less. [The differences in feelings brought on by the two kinds of waiting were dumbfounding.]

Pregnancy comes with visible signs of physical progress.

Adopting doesn't. [Or at least it wasn't supposed to. But having just moved back to the States after having dreamed for months about what, where, and with whom I would be eating, I was beginning to show. Concern really spiked when my jokes about being the pregnant one started drawing double takes.]

Pregnancy is not something you can hurry. People sell prenatal Mozart with promises of heightened intelligence, but nobody is throwing research dollars at experiments to reduce gestation to a more convenient, say, 25 weeks. No, the process is what it is, wholly necessary, and you cannot hurry it.

Adopting, on the other hand, has many points at which you might try to influence or hurry the process. You could switch programs. You could switch countries. You could widen the scope of special needs you will accept. When there is a snag in the process of dealing with multiple agencies across separate governments in two countries, the solution might be a simple workaround orchestrated within the adoption agency. Or maybe phoning your senator. Perhaps someone else is a candidate for a personal visit or a forceful conversation or a bribe. None of Tammy's pregnancies required us to make decisions on best practices with any of those options. And in adoption they are all extreme exceptions. What is

23

generally required and universally expected from the waiting family is only that. Waiting. Hurry up and wait.

Pregnancy cannot be slowed down. Barring something tragic, the process that began with conception will inexorably march forward toward birth. The "Honey, I think we should wait two years until I'm finished with my PhD program" conversation must take place before the pregnancy or not at all. There is no pause button and there are no two-year pregnancies.

Adopting can always be slowed down, ostensibly at the drop of any kind of hat you can conceive of. [We were forever waiting for news of this or that piece of paper. When the expected time of receipt for one came and went, we could only stab at possible explanations: Was it languishing somewhere on someone's desk? Why? What if they were eating at their desk and spilled General Tso on it? What if it fell off the desk? What if it was lying in the crack between the desk and the wall? Reality quickly evaporated to make room for fantasy.]

Pregnancy is understandable by everybody. Which is understandable, as it has been around since, well, everybody. A majority of earth's women will experience pregnancy. Many men live through one under their roof. Everyone has watched a mom or a sister or a cousin or a neighbor progress through its stages. We don't remember being in our own mother's womb, but it isn't long afterwards that we know what growing bellies are all about. It's common and normal, even if it is miraculous.

Adopting, on the other hand, is poorly understood by most, unless they've experienced adoption themselves.

Before we started our adoption process, I understood nothing.

. . . .

I was still ignorant. And a thousand leagues from knowing how irrelevant my fathering experience so far would ultimately prove to be. But at least there in the waiting process I had game: sitting around was something I excelled at. Good thing, because we did a lot of it that spring, mostly behind the wheel of our borrowed silver minivan. We were home from China and had a lot of people to see. From California to Pennsylvania to Minnesota to Texas.

And it was on that Texas leg, a thousand miles from our temporary home in Indiana, eight thousand miles from our semipermanent home in China, that Lily Day came. With that one phone call our family went from five to six. One orphan, one day parentless and nearly forgotten, the next beloved and wanted. Complete and unlooked-for redemption. We thought it was cool that, as we would soon return to China, she wouldn't even have to leave her time zone to join our family. Our agency said if everything proceeded normally, we could expect to get her in two to five months. Nice range. But our return flights to China were in two, so it was perfect.

Just About There

BUT UPON OUR RETURN to China, things had not followed the timetable we'd envisioned.

At all.

Though we had hoped and assumed we would finalize by the end of summer, our actual adoption pickup date was delayed by months. A time came when we succumbed to hoping and praying for an adoptive union by Christmas. Our agency warned us that even that was overly optimistic.

The final unlooked-for delay was some unexplained holdup with our Letter of Acceptance. The entire month of November went by with no visible progress or news. The date our agency had expected the LOA came and went. "Frustrating" edged toward frantic. We were headed to Thailand in January and therefore felt ourselves reasonable and qualified candidates for expediting (as surely everyone who asks for special treatment does). But we weren't even getting documents by normal process deadlines.

We were so discouraged. Since it was out of our hands, we decided to focus on something that wasn't. When our LOA did arrive in all its red-stamped glory, instead of signing and overnight-ing it back to the U.S., only to have it placed in a pile to await the next agency shipment back to China again, I hand-delivered it to our agency's Beijing office myself. They in turn submitted it to the China Center for Children's Welfare and Adoption (CCCWA⁶) the same day. All told, we saved several days, maybe even a week or more, time in which Travel Approval—TA, our final paperwork step—could move forward. The round trip train ticket to Beijing had not even cost much more than one overnight envelope to the States.

In Beijing I had the privilege of meeting the staff and our agency's in-country director. Now I would have faces and smiles to picture in all future interactions.

Two short weeks after my visit, the director sent us the most enjoyable text message we'd ever gotten. It came, we tearfully observed as a sign that God had not forgotten us, on Christmas Day.

The text read, "TA has arrived. You can go get her."

Our daughter was in Guangzhou. When Tammy and I arrived in that city for the very first time, our excitement was off the charts. The wait was over. The day had come. Tomorrow we would meet her.

It had been a long time since Tammy and I had been on a trip just the two of us. We enjoyed a leisurely dinner out before returning to our room at the Guangzhou White Swan Hotel. This was before a subsequent major remodel, so we saw it much as it had been for the visits of numerous dignitaries, including U.S. presidents and Queen Elizabeth. One could feel the history, not only of the famous, but of the many adoptive families who had stayed there, too.

We went to bed like wide-eyed six-year-olds on Christmas Eve, doubtful sleep would ever come. In the morning, we went down to the buffet for our last breakfast as the parents of three. Midmorning found us in a taxi on our way to the building where families are changed forever. They told us our daughter was on her way, too. We were escorted to a second floor room with a row of new-looking couches against the far wall. The seat cushions were scarlet, the backrests a jumble of shapes in black and white. The ceilings were low.

Good grief, I'm nervous—I am noticing everything. Where is she? How long will we have to wait? Should I start the video camera? "How are you doing, dear? Isn't this so weird feeling? Our daughter is going to come in through that door!"

I have no memory that remotely compares to what it was like to sit on a newish black and white and red-all-over couch waiting for strangers in an adjacent low-ceilinged room to carry out a little girl I would easily recognize, that I already called daughter, already loved, but had never seen.

While we waited, other children were brought out to other

waiting families. All girls that day. All different ages. Some with visible special needs, some without. Some met their new families with a smile, some did not. One kicked and screamed and clung to her caregiver. Another came out running and shouting, "Mom and Dad!" She'd gotten their photo album.

One by one the parents met their new daughters in tears.

A realization (so, so blind) that we'd finally reached the end of adoption difficulty flitted through my head.

We were given the signal. Ours was next.

Surgery and More Screaming

THE STORY WILL COME back to those couches soon, but first a word on just how brutal it was scheduling our daughter for cleft palate surgery on the heels of bringing her home. For indeed there is no other solution for a cleft palate but surgery. So, being down (with the screaming and desperation of those first weeks), we decided we might as well give ourselves a swift kick, too: let's not just have an inconsolable child unable to receive comfort, let's have an inconsolable child in great physical pain unable to receive comfort.

Not actually.

In truth we'd had little choice in the surgery's timing. We were already scheduled for a trip to Thailand and its world-class hospitals.

Every year our family did medical appointments in Thailand, and happily. But this year, the only enjoyable part about our hospital stay happened to be the food. Not the taste per se, mind you (it was above-average cafeteria food), but the hoot of figuring out why I had been liking it and Tammy hadn't. Each night, one of us had slept at the hospital while the other slept at our Bangkok guesthouse with the rest of the kids. We traded off each day, and didn't overlap at all until the last day. I was in the room just before checkout when Tammy's last meal arrived. "Do you always choose Chinese?" I asked her.

"What do you mean, 'choose Chinese'? I've never chosen anything, they just cart this stuff in." I saw immediately what had been going on. She'd been given her food automatically, while I had been given a little menu each meal. I could choose between Western, Chinese, Thai, or Halal. We love Chinese, but my motivation to eat it—in an institution, prepared by non-Chinese, when my home was China—was nil. Likewise, had I wanted Thai, or even Middle Eastern, I'd have gone out to the street. Bangkok food options are out of this world. In the hospital I stuck with Western.

The underlying culprit, remarkably, was hair. My blond wife was not currently blond. Back in China she'd told all our friends that she would signal the news we had been informed we could go meet our daughter by dyeing her hair black. And now, as the Thai staff figured *one* of us had to have produced this Chinese baby, it must be black-haired Mom. Tammy should have been clued in the first day when the nursing staff (who communicated just fine in English) brought a Chinese staff member to her room. Unsure why, Tammy talked with him in Mandarin for a few minutes until it dawned on her that he was a translator—the staff had assumed she couldn't speak English. She and the translator shared a laugh together, but Tammy never did make a connection between that episode and the meals she was being brought.

Nothing else about the ordeal was funny. For three weeks following the surgery, we had to keep the poor stitched-throated patient in removable arm casts to prevent her from sticking anything in her mouth. Onto an already intractable situation, the casts piled discomfort, heat, and annoyance. They only came off for quick baths, and while one of us washed, the other made sure a baby who was desperate to suck and chew didn't slip anything into her mouth. Her diet was strictly liquid, and no bottles, not even a rubber spoon, were allowed. Every drop went in by syringe. Our already threadbare willingness to deal with Miss Fuss wore thinner still.

We managed to stave off a complete unraveling long enough to outlast the three-week ban on solid foods. Only to be demoralized as she staunchly refused, or was unable, to swallow. Some bites, in spite of our best efforts at encouragement and cheering and throat massage, did nothing but liquefy in her mouth until we let her spit them out thirty minutes later. Every meal, either Tammy or I would be at the table for hours.

The screaming fits wore on.

We came home to China from surgery and vacation in Thailand never having been more in need of a vacation in our lives. In the girls' room we placed a length of foam on the floor next to the crib. Every night either Tammy, exhausted from daytime Ergototing sessions, or I, exhausted from nightly screaming sessions, would fall asleep there. We slept with our hands through the slats, big fingers gripped by little ones. Some nights nothing worked. Some nights nothing stopped the screaming. Nothing comforted her.

Sometimes we got just plain sick of her.

But we trudged on, three hours at a time. It wasn't screaming the whole three hours every night. There wasn't screaming at nap time every single day. But we couldn't leave the room before deep sleep, either. That was what she was afraid of: us leaving. The screaming was fear. Terror. Pure terror that closing her eyes might mean no one would be there when she opened them. Not even dozing off could rob her of her wariness. She would automatically wake every so often to make a visual check. If we were still lying on the floor next to the crib, if our fingers were still reaching though the slats and touching hers, her heavy eyelids would fall back in place. But if we were not there, or if our fingers were not inside the crib, she screamed.

Life became an extended stretch of all-time lows.

Back to the Future

And the Princess Birthday Party

I GO TO THE window and look twelve floors down again. There's the pink dress, heading up the path.

The three-year-old birthday princess who has transformed before our very eyes is on her way up. She's stopping at every flower to let her shutterbug shadow take one last shot of one last pose. Okay, one more.

After I arrange the cupcakes into a giant '3' on a platter, they each get a candle. Matches stand at the ready. I whistle for our other three kids and the four guests who have arrived while the Princess is out. They all crowd around in a dining room decorated with Belle, Aurora, Cinderella, and everything princess. I flash the cupcake plate to a cacophony of squeals and a bunch of feigned drooling.

The Princess is in the elevator. We hold our breath.

"Get ready to sing big, kids!"

. . . .

Princesses have been big at our house since Haddie came on the scene. But amid all the dressing up, all the play, and everything princess she ever did, one memory rises to eclipse them all: the day Haddie met Cinderella. A picture of the moment is on proud display in her room.

The picture was taken at Disney World, a surprise trip for our kids from Tammy's folks, and practically the first place we went after returning from our first stint in western China. For weeks leading up to our trip, five-year-old Haddie placidly, patiently, and persistently parried all parental pointers about prickly heat, pain, pangs, and impracticality, not to mention paternal preferences for not looking like weirdos: she insisted she would like to wear her Cinderella dress the whole day. With mom's secret encouragement, she outlasted me. I said fine.

On the big day, we parked the van somewhere near sunup. From a lot named, appropriately, Goofy, we began traversing the remaining leagues to the park in fully half the modes of transportation known to man. The closer we got to the gate, the more China-sized the crowds got. After four years of not having seen so many as a hundred non-Asians together in one place, it was a little like standing on top of a churning avalanche. Like Mulan had just shot a canon at the nearest snowy mountain. We flailed to keep our footing.

Then there it was: Main Street, USA.

Invisible forces went to work on our little party immediately, steering us in an automated speed walk toward the princess meet and greet. My head was on a swivel, staring down anyone looking like they might try to pass us. To my dismay, however, we were nothing like the first to arrive. At least four thousand other people had had better invisible forces, or must have camped there overnight. For there they stood, bleating in lines of staggering length.

Look at all the little girls. The only chance Haddie had had of looking weird would have been to *not* wear her Cinderella dress. I was an unenlightened father, indeed. Small surprise, I suppose, from a guy who had to have a daughter before learning there simply weren't any princesses named Sleeping Beauty.

Silly daddy, I told you.

The blat of an internal alarm interrupted—this place had all the earmarks of a cult. It was time to convert or get out. I got out. Grandparents were there to be the hero for my daughter that day. I couldn't stand in one of those stupefying lines; I questioned whether Haddie could hack it. It turns out I was unenlightened about that, too. It wouldn't have mattered to her if they had stretched back to the van.

Was it worth it?

One look at the picture is all that's needed. I never tire of gazing at Haddie's face in that picture. Of staring at her adulation

for a Princess she does not realize is an actress:
You're really Cinderella.
I'm looking at you, Cinderella.
Do you like my dress? I mean your dress? I mean this dress on me that's my Cinderella dress?
I like you, you're my favorite.
I'm smiling. I'm smiling at you. I can't feel my face.
But that's OK, because you're Cinderella. May I smile at you some more?
Oh, it was worth it.

. . . .

On that day, those princesses were Real.

Like her sister is Real, now. She is Real to all of us. It boggles our minds to look back on how far this former orphan has come. Some difficulties seem far away and long ago. The difficulties that remain are less difficult. The difficulties yet ahead do not affect us. We can hardly remember our lives without her. Our affection for her ever grows.

The doorbell rings. I light the candles, and a kid throws open the door. Tammy brings the wide-eyed birthday girl around the corner to a thrilling view of friends singing and chocolate blazing. I can see the candles reflecting in her eyes.

Happy birthday to you,
Happy birthday to you,
Happy birthday, dear Eden,
Happy birthday to you!

Eden. Yes, Eden. This precious girl, our beloved, adopted, though we seldom include that second adjective, daughter—the one with the überpersonality whose doting siblings and parents have been loving her for almost two years—is not Lily.

The girl we fell in love with first…has never come home.

Lily Anne is still an orphan.

Part II

Loss

Sick

病来如山倒

Sickness comes like an avalanche

Chinese saying

SHE'D BEEN ILL FROM the beginning.

Before the beginning.

The day we parked alongside the road to take the referral call, Lily was already sick. They'd matched us with a child with an unknown malady. No child with an undiagnosed sickness is ever matched with a family. Severe special needs, physical abnormalities, and medical conditions of all kinds, yes—none of these prevent adoption. But everything has been diagnosed, documented, and delineated in the paperwork. Conversely, it is always also possible for health problems to arise after a match. But matching a family with a sick, undiagnosed child is unheard of.

Our agency was not to blame; they didn't know Liu Hai Rou was sick. The China side, CCCWA, was not to blame; they didn't know either. Only her own small orphanage knew, and they had failed to pass the word up the line. And so a very sick little girl, who under normal circumstances would never have been matched with anyone, was matched with us. By Lily Day she had already been to the hospital twice. A week after Lily Day she went again. She was vomiting. There was no diagnosis. And no one notified the CCCWA.

Meanwhile, juggling preparations for returning to China, we showed off pictures of a precious daughter to everyone in sight.

. . . .

We'd been matched for some weeks when it came time to submit our Five Questions. Each family is allowed to ask their waiting child's orphanage five questions. The agency collects them, the CCCWA approves them, and the orphanage answers them. Or doesn't.

People attach immense hope to these questions. Any kind of information about the daily life of your child is golden. We had some China orphanage experience that made us more aware than most what Lily's life may have been like, but we were as hungry for specifics as anyone. Pictures are the best of all. Each one might represent months or even years of life. We typed our questions and requests for pictures into an email. But our excitement was ill-fated. We never heard back.

The day we sent them was Lily's first birthday.

Lily Anne was mere months from becoming a Johnson, but that day she felt far, far away. A baby turns one once. The irretrievability of that loss hit Tammy particularly hard because with our other three she had done photo shoots at a studio, pitting each diapered birthday baby against a cake on the floor. Enoch was tentative. Haddie took a dive, never quit grinning. Elijah parried, thrust, and lunged, then cried. Lily...wasn't here.

Had she the best caregivers in the world, it still would have felt wrong that we weren't the ones celebrating the day with her. We knew orphanage life precluded being able to celebrate every child's birthday, but we wondered if those around her even knew. Would Liu Hai Rou's birth date slip by without anyone marking the day for her?

. . . .

Reality was far worse. Lily's birthday meal was liquids, taken intravenously to deter vomiting.

. . . .

Lily had been sick before we were matched, but she had not yet been Lily. It was the match that had triggered our settling on a name. It had actually been eight years since we'd had reason to discuss girl names. We'd found out Elijah's sex ahead of time, so during that pregnancy we'd known we only needed a boy name, and already had it left over from when Haddie had turned out to be a girl.

Nor had we discussed girl names for Haddie (full name Hadassa, a blend of Persian Queen Esther's Hebrew name, Hadassah, and Tammy's great grandmother's, Hadessa). Hers was left over from when our firstborn had turned out to be a son. So, we had no girl names in reserve when Lily came along. We were hoping to continue our tradition of using some combination of Old Testament and family names, but did toy with some others as well. We gave serious consideration to carrying over a Chinese character or two from Liu Hai Rou, but as that name was only assigned by orphanage administration and not given by birth parents or anyone who loved her, we chose not to. She would be getting a new informal Chinese name anyway, as all our kids have. In the end, we loved the beauty and purity represented by the name Lily in the Song of Solomon passages[7] we took it from. Her middle name, Anne,[8] came from both sides of our family tree.

But of all our baby-naming experiences, the most convoluted had been the choice for our firstborn's. Months ahead of time we were all prepared with girl and boy selections, first and middle. Then, all through the pregnancy, we heard of a friend here, an acquaintance there, eventually more people than we could stand, using the boy's name we had chosen. Maybe we were being ridiculous, but we felt compelled to make a change. Being a Johnson from the Midwest made the desire for a unique name feel like more than preference.

That summer my parents came down from Chicago to roast with us in Texas. After one of our baby-shopping trips together, we were driving home and discussing boy names over the roar of the air conditioner. The July due date loomed. We had nothing. As a humorous diversion, I threw in a family name we would never dream of using. Aanuk.

Aanuk was my great uncle. He and my maternal grandmother were two of eleven children raised on a small farmstead in Leland, Norway. My grandmother was sixteen when she emigrated from

Norway, traveling alone on an Atlantic steamer to begin a new life in a Norwegian community in New Jersey.[9] Each month she sent home a portion of her earnings from working as a governess. Norway was a poor country, not yet having drilled the riches of North Sea oil. Some years later, my grandmother received a letter from home telling her that the farm could no longer support even the family who remained. Her parents were going to have to send one of the two remaining girls to Kristiansand, seventy kilometers away, to look for work. Aanuk, age seventeen, had already gone to sea.

He worked on the Norwegian merchant ships that plied the North Atlantic shipping lanes connecting North America with Europe and the Soviet Union. On one trip to New York he made a surreptitious visit to his sister, my grandmother, now with a family of her own, in New Jersey. He jumped ship to do it, so perhaps planned to stay for some time. It wasn't long before immigration officials showed up on my grandparents' doorstep. They extracted Aanuk from his not-so-stellar hiding place under the kitchen table and returned him to his ship. Sail to Canada, they advised him, then immigrate from there. It was the last piece of advice anyone ever gave him.

. . . .

I stop at a red light.

"Mom, how do you spell Uncle Aanuk's name, anyway?"

"Well, you know, the same as in Genesis: 'e-n-o-c-h' or wait, I think his ended with a 'k' instead."

"What, are you serious? You mean that Uncle Aanuk is really Uncle Enoch?"

"Of course, you never knew that? It's just the Norwegian pronunciation of 'e-n-o-c-h' that sounds like 'Aanuk.'"

"Man, I never knew that."

The car idles. I turn the air down a smidge. The light turns.

Tammy and I shout at once: "Enoch!"

An Old Testament name, a family name, and an uncommon name all wrapped in one.

. . . .

Great Uncle Enok did spell his name with a 'k,' and in the middle of January, 1942, he left New York on the D/S Belize, bound for St. John's in Canada. He never made it. The Belize sank on January 21, the first torpedo kill of type-VIIC U-boat U-754 in Germany's just-launched U-boat offensive. Of the wreckage, nothing was found save (eventually) one water-filled lifeboat holding four dead seamen. Enok Leland, age eighteen years and two months, was not one of them.

My own mother was not yet born when the tragedy occurred, but her oldest brother Werner is old enough to remember. My Uncle Werner[10] was five years old when Enok's ship went down. He came home from school to find my young grandmother in tears at the ironing board, pressing the day's wash as the news about her brother sank in.

Fifty years later—minus one day—on January 20, I would have my first date with the girl who would become my wife. More years would pass, and Tammy and I, on our mad search for a replacement name for our firstborn, would happily stumble upon Great Uncle's.

To use if we had a boy.

For only *boys* are given the name Enoch.

Or at least I had thought so.

. . . .

Our visit home to the U.S. from China was winding down.

We knew nothing of Lily's symptoms, but they were consistent: choking and gagging on her food, regular vomiting. No doctor provided a diagnosis. No one could say what was wrong with her, even as her condition deteriorated.

Really Sick

But now I have a heart I cannot keep
And the greatest of fear
is that you'll leave me here
Stranded in this water so deep

Bebo Norman, "In Your Hands"

A YEAR HOME IS no visit; it's a move. Going back to China would be another one, so that made two moves in one year. Packing a family for a move to a foreign country is no fun. The decisions never end: what to give away, what to put in storage, what to store at mom's for easy access or someone to bring later, what to sell at the garage sale, how to unload the astonishing amount of junk that accumulates in such a short time, how many sticks of deodorant to bring for the years ahead, how many sizes of kids' clothing and shoes it's worth bringing when weighed against higher prices and lower quality in China, what size clothes to bring for Lily, which locally unavailable children's medications to bring, how to arrange final goodbyes to family and friends...on and on and on they went.

And there was more than just packing to worry about. We had dental appointments for five and we needed to schedule at least that many appointments for shots. Haddie came down with the vomiting flu in the van on the final leg of our road trip, so, once home, we quarantined her and kept the boys outside as much as possible. Then Enoch fell on the playground, and I agreed with his cool self-diagnosis—"I broke my arm"—with one nauseating glance at the deep "V" between his elbow and wrist. The doctor who set the bones gave us only marginal hope that the cast could come off before our departure for China.

Throughout it all, Lily filled our minds. The end was in sight. We counted down the days until our flight. Upcoming was the Letter of Acceptance, and after that, Travel Approval. TA would mean we could start counting down the days until picking up Lily.

It so happened our flight back fell on our thirteenth wedding anniversary. As the main flight was thirteen hours as well, I told Tammy I'd had to search high and low for an anniversary gift of such lucky, romantic coincidence. Obviously, she swooned.

Completing our joy, the kids were seven, five, and just-turned two, that final age quite possibly the worst one of all for a trip of such length. Flying for any length of time with young children is never a walk in the park. But make it a flight long enough for beverage service, snacks, dinner, a whole night's sleep, and breakfast, and you're really rolling the dice. Anything can happen. Except get that whole night's sleep. That won't happen.

Some flights with young children, especially those over oceans, seem like they'll never end. And not just to parents. What frequent flyer doesn't have war stories about some kid's inconsolable wailing, fussing fit, or mischievous kicking? No brand of that misery, however, can compare with *being* the helpless parent struggling to soothe exhausted, hungry, or restless children on flights long enough to flip body clocks upside down.

People who have never flown with small children in tow cannot possibly understand how different air travel without them can be from air travel with them. I have overheard childless travelers so incensed over mere delay that they administered a public dressing-down of whatever airline employee happened to be nearby. Look, I'm not saying that being mercilessly stranded for two endless hours of magazine browsing and latte sipping isn't rough. But until someone has traveled with more suitcases than they have fingers, or run through a terminal with a vomiting child, or been that parent with the inconsolable baby, or had diarrhea soil their shirt an hour from the nearest restroom, they simply don't know what they're talking about.

In-flight life for the parent of young ones is indiscernible from that of a carnival whack-a-mole. Up. Down. Up. Down. Up. Down. An airplane somehow winds a child's neediness just a tad bit tighter. And hands their parents that disagreeable task of marshaling the same back-and-forth parade that's robbing them of full-price seats. I'd welcome a good whack from a flight attendant with a padded mallet if it kept us in our seats. On some long hauls we've been in absentia for so long we've had to shoo away one or two of those seat roamers who'd left the crowdedness of their own row to plop down in the mistaken emptiness of ours. Who knows how our litter of toys, snacks, clothes, and shoes hadn't clued them in.

We were ready for the move back to China. As we got on the plane, not even the usual looks of fear from passengers who were worried that our one-ring circus would sit in their row could dampen our spirits now. Lily was near. Our other kids had bags of snacks, games, and wrapped trinkets prepared by mom. Even better, every seat had movie and gaming screens, a first for us. Our kids were excited about returning to the one place in the world that was more home to them than anywhere else. All through packing we had giggled at their happy shrieks over suddenly-remembered stuffed animals waiting for them in China, or a long-missed Lego set.

We stowed the carry-ons, got the kids settled, and sat back to enjoy what would be home for the next thirteen romantic hours. Then, just as we had five years earlier, we left American soil behind. I gazed at my three beautiful children: they were worth effortless traveling days being over.

We could hardly wait for number four.

We ached for those few low-resolution photos of Lily to materialize into the real girl. We longed to experience her personality, to learn her likes and her dislikes. What was happening in her life that month? What was going on that very day? There were so many fun details we didn't know.

. . . .

She was in the hospital for the fifth time, and her third hospital stay had lasted ten full days. Her stool and her vomit were filled with blood.

. . . .

After wrangling our thirteen-hour anniversary celebration, we slung fifteen bags up to our temporary housing. Thinking we would save ourselves work, and shored up by the motto "dig neatly," we established the hysterical policy of keeping all suitcases packed for the next few days. We lost that battle, but hardly cared due to the war we were losing at night. Twelve-hour jet lag plays unspeakable tricks on the minds and bodies of small children.

We had to find housing fast. We were moving back to China, but not to the city where we had lived before we left. Everything from our former apartment would need a place to land in one week. We were elated when we found a place in two days.

We flew to our old city to pack three trucks with the stuff a family of five accumulates over four years. We had no choice but to all five go—expatriates are generally minus grandparents, other family, and handy long-term friends to leave children with. Once there, Tammy worked in the apartment while I traveled around to settle accounts with the bank, TV service company, electric company, phone company, apartment complex, and landlord; and in between we fit in dinners to bid farewell to friends.

We finished packing up the apartment just as three small moving trucks arrived. We supervised the loading, then beat it to the airport for our flight back. The next day I did the reverse of the rounds I had just done, traipsing around to turn on phone, internet, electricity, gas, and water. When the trucks made it twenty-some hours later and started unloading our things, some of it so covered in road dust we hardly recognized it. Inevitably something was going to be broken, too. We'd been through this before.

The last time we'd moved within China, I'd handled the broken-stuff negotiations. That was a mistake. The very last item that had been loaded on that truck (our family had been small enough to need only one) had been a large framed photo of the Great Wall. Instead of loading it north south between mattresses or anything protective, the movers had loaded it east to west, right up against the truck's back door. Before the door even closed, I laughed and told the head guy the picture was going to break. I could have predicted his response in my sleep: "No problem, there should be no problem."

"Okay, but why don't we open the truck and move it anyway?"

"No need, our company has a guarantee. It's not a worry."

I'd chosen this company because of that guarantee. It's true: I was comforted by it. Had I known how it worked, I would not have been.

Sure enough, on the other end of the move, the frame was

cracked. When the truck was finally empty at two in the morning, I only wanted to go to bed. But we had to take care of the damage compensation first. *Just cut me the reimbursement check already and get out of here.* Who knows what I was expecting.

That's when I learned the nature of the moving company's "guarantee." First, I wouldn't get a dime unless I fought them tooth and nail for it. Second, I would have to extract it, not from the company, but from the salaries of the laborers. My head spun as I watched the head man's about-face. His "not to worries" were now groveling and whining. Couldn't I appreciate the gap between our economic statuses? Surely, he contended, such incidentals could not be as important to me as it was for him and his workers to be able to take home their meager salaries.

The fact that I had pointed out the frame explicitly? Been given patently empty assurances about its safety? Didn't faze him one bit. He shrewdly threw all his eggs into the basket of my mercy.

I folded like a napkin.

Not this time, not on this move. This time around, Tammy would be the negotiator. She was not susceptible to pitiful tactics, and she wouldn't be spinelessly taken advantage of. As our three trucks had been loaded, she'd taken charge. Items loaded carelessly? She'd told them to slow down. Without proper wrapping? She'd pointed it out. But for the most part she'd gotten the same "Not a problem!" replies that I had years earlier. Then, of course, on the other end now, some of those very same things were damaged. But none so bad that the workers thought it anything worth mentioning. Tammy stood her ground. And out came the same ploy that had been used on me. It was unkind, they implied, for people wealthy enough to ship three trucks from another province to expect a company to actually stand behind a guarantee when the sting of that guarantee fell upon the backs of its workers, who after all have such very low salaries.

Man, they are so right… I fold.

Not so fast. Tammy, with superior wisdom—and, I might add, compassion—waded right in, more at home in the Chinese negotiation arena than I'll ever be.

"No," she insisted back to the workers, "I told you how to do it right, you refused, and it broke. If we don't keep you accountable for doing better work than that, how are we helping the next customer? Your salary being low is all the more reason you should have listened to me. It's your own fault you didn't listen, and if I let you off the hook, you're going to turn around and ignore the next customer, too, which only bodes poorly for your company. Really, if you look at it the right way, I'm helping you."[11]

The debate went back and forth spiritedly during the last few loads and over half an hour. Tammy bent on the amount of her fines but would not break, and in the end they had no choice but to cave. I thought they'd resent her inflexibility, only to gape as their whining turned to praise and they started complimenting her good bargaining skills. They left smiling.

I don't know how to talk price about anything.

A week after our move, Enoch turned eight, and we squeezed in a quick dinosaur party with his friends. Then we continued putting up shelving, assembling furniture, arranging and rearranging everything until everyone—two parents, two boys, and soon-to-be-two girls—fit. Haddie turned six. Of course there was a princess party as the Cinderella photo had been just the year before. We cleaned up from that party and took our first evening off in over a month. Almost finished. So close to a routine life (other than the minor detail that we were about to adopt) that we went to bed dreaming about it.

The next morning, the phone service came on. This meant the internet was on, too, so no more office wifi runs. I ran to the computer to check email. I'd been checking religiously for weeks. My heart skipped a beat: finally, it had come. We, along with a select group of other families, were being told to prepare for travel.

Travel Approval, the final hurdle. We had worked so hard and waited so pins-and-needly for so long, it hardly seemed real.

We jumped around the house for joy. Our eyes shone knowing we'd soon be Lily's mom and dad for real. Big brothers and big sister were jumping, too.

· · · ·

The pictures we continued to excitedly share of a fat, happy baby were every day looking a little less like the real girl.

She was beginning to starve. No one knew why.

· · · ·

47

I was back at the computer later that morning and saw a second email from the agency. Not a group one like the first, but a personal one.

> Hi, Dann and Tammy,
> Can you please let me know, again, how to reach you by phone?
> We have an update on your child.
> Thanks,
> Rebecca Makos
> Director of Adoption Services

Rebecca was already off work and home for the evening back in the States, so we had all day on China time to chat about what her news might be. Though her email was a bit stark, we weren't worried. The tone of my reply was light:

> Hi, Rebecca!
> Great news in Darwin's email to us! TA!
> I've attached our land line number. You can call us before you leave work.
> Tammy is looking forward to this first chance to speak with you.
> The Johnsons
> Dann, Tammy, Enoch, Haddie, Elijah, Lily

I'd long since made that adjustment to our email signature.

The next morning dawned hot and sunny. Our kids stirred early, ready for another day of summer play. We were still in bed when the phone rang.

And our lives changed.

I recognized the same voice that had announced she "had a little girl" for us. Now that voice knocked the wind from us with the aberrant news that Lily was ill.

How very odd.

"Is it serious?"

Rebecca had little information other than the blood in Lily's vomit and stool. How long it had been going on she didn't know. She'd just been told herself, and seemed troubled at getting such mysterious news so late in the process. She would get more information as soon as she could.

Rebecca couldn't guess what Lily's illness would mean for the adoption. But we no longer had approval for traveling, that was plain. TA was withdrawn. Our process was frozen until they could figure out what was wrong. Rebecca sincerely apologized for narrowly missing the cutoff time for the Travel Approval email the day before and not preventing this emotional roller coaster. Indeed, it would mean failing to prevent all downstream processes, as even our official TA hard copy would arrive at our front door a few days later via international courier. It would be meaningless.

Rebecca had a second reason she needed to speak with us: no one assumed families necessarily desired to keep such a match. If we preferred, the CCCWA could accommodate us with a rematch. No waiting. And no one would think any less of us. With Liu Hai Rou, the road ahead was a complete unknown. If Rebecca believed a new match was preferable—it would still lead to joy and blessing for us and for a child—she didn't say it. We felt no pressure. She just needed a decision.

I could hear myself advising someone else: "You have no idea what type of illness this girl has. It could be anything. You will grow to love another." But I didn't feel that way. We could not "move on" from Lily. It was far too soon to speak of abandoning her, even if that wasn't the word anyone used. This girl was not "some orphan"— she had parents. And they wanted her, maybe now more than ever.

We were clear. "Tell the CCCWA we'll wait. Do whatever it takes to facilitate completing the adoption. In fact," we wondered aloud, "why not allow us to fly or train or drive to her right now? We could be there in a day." We had TA. Was anybody going to deny that a family's care would provide her the absolute best chances for recovery?

Rebecca promised to press for more information and to advocate for us. She also forwarded us the in-house email that had broken the news of Lily's sickness to her. She would keep us in that loop from then on, and we were fortunate to have the direct window onto agency communication. Since we spoke the language and knew the culture, I could sometimes back-translate the English emails of Chinese staff and discern a meaning more accurate than I got from reading their English only. I saw we'd have lost a lot if we'd only gotten summaries, so we were grateful.

From that first forwarded email we realized that Lily's orphanage had been as blindsided by the news Liu Hai Rou had a family as we had been by her sickness. A very sick girl in their legal care had been matched three months earlier, and somehow they didn't know. They'd now asked the CCCWA to cancel everything and return the child's file to them. But things would not be so simple with a foreign agency and a family involved. The CCCWA, not the orphanage, held the power.

But the CCCWA could not satisfy both parties. Would they give any weight to what we wanted? Our desires stood in direct opposition to what the orphanage director wanted. For him, the worst case scenario would be the CCCWA failing to give him back the file, and face. For us, the worst case scenario would be Lily's health deteriorating so much that the CCCWA deemed her unadoptable. For Lily, the worst case scenario would be her caregivers deeming her beyond their ability to help.[12]

A day went by. No more news. Two days. Three. We were numb. Our three children had to eat, so that meant keeping up some kind of routine, but we could not stave off a creeping irritability with regular life. We had gone from celebrating TA, the supposed end of waiting, to not only waiting again, but to the worst kind of waiting. Tammy likened her anguish to that of finding out about the possibility of imminent miscarriage. Waiting before had had steps that people spelled out for you. This waiting was a black hole of the unknowable. We didn't know what we were waiting for. No one knew when the waiting would end. No one knew how things would end.

We were helpless.

Roller-coastering

DETAILS ABOUT LILY'S SICKNESS trickled to our inbox. We learned just how long she'd been sick. From our third-hand reading we patched together various theories about what might be wrong. More, we tried to guess what motivated the CCCWA and would be influencing their decisions. They asked our agency what we wanted.

Why were they repeating themselves? We'd told them. We wanted Lily. It would have been simpler for everyone had we volunteered to drop the match then and there, but we weren't giving up that quickly. We spoke at length on the phone with Rebecca, telling her we needed a diagnosis before anyone could expect us to speak of other matches. Why could not Liu Hai Rou be taken to the children's hospital in the provincial capital for an MRI, more blood tests? What if Lily's issues were easily correctable after an accurate diagnosis? From the emails we could see that this was the line of reasoning our agency had already been using with the CCCWA. They had been telling them that taking Lily to the big city hospital was the only right thing to do. We hoped the CCCWA would find that morally compelling, but we didn't know. We knew the paths of moral obligation wound very differently in the two cultures.

The CCCWA's actual next step was quintessentially Chinese. They widened the collaboration. We didn't know if them bringing in the Civil Affairs office from Lily's province was good news or not, but we chose to call it that and began pipe-dreaming about some advantage, some compassionate person with power, that might materialize out of Civil Affairs.

51

We could see that the attention Liu Hai Rou was getting was a direct result of our match. Without us, they might have given up on her already. We continued to press for the visit to a bigger hospital; our agency had already said they could staff the trip. They could stay with her at the hospital.[13] They would be willing to cover all costs. But it had to be soon. Lily's condition was grave.

. . . .

The orphanage director was insistent. They could handle all medical needs by themselves. They could take the child to the big city if necessary. But twice during these very negotiations Liu Hai Rou had been hospitalized, received no diagnosis, and not been taken elsewhere. The failure to reach a diagnosis made us want to pull our hair out, and the frequency of hospital visits was becoming alarming. At first it seemed good that at least they were taking her, and we had no reason to suspect any motive other than returning Liu Hai Rou to full health. But as the situation crept on, the director's decisions made less and less sense. Now he claimed that the child could not be transferred anywhere. She had never been in a vehicle, so was unfit to travel. We were over a week into the negotiations, and there had been no progress. What was going on? Why were they taking her over and over to the hospital, giving the appearance of care, but unwilling to take the next step?

Anxiety over losing her spiked. The possibility of a coming letdown grew so real that we were forced to mull over our options in case we lost her. Tammy and I disagreed over how hard to push the agency. My practicality took over. I insisted we maintain some measure of professionalism. I loved Lily, but that didn't mean I had to act unreasonably. Tammy was far more attached. This was her daughter. What were appearance and reasonableness compared to that? She cared about Lily, not what the agency thought. Of course I agreed Lily was our daughter, but there wasn't anyone else who saw her that way. I wasn't going to cross the line of overreaction. I would act reasonably. No one was going to think of me as a crazy person.

Aunt Tammy,
Lately I have been thinking a lot about Lily and I really wanted to feel like I knew her, and thus hurt with you. I longed to under-

stand this all and feel close to her like you guys. Then I had a dream. I was at your house. Lily was there and I wanted to play with her, but she just kept wanting only you and Dann. I was sad about this in my dream, but when I woke up it now felt like I knew her personally. I had seen her face, and she was so real.

I feel so much more connected with her and really long to get to know her for real. I miss you guys and I am thinking of and praying for you often!

Love you lots!

Carrie

P.S. I really felt led to tell you this dream. I think God wanted me to share that He gave it to me so you would know He is with you.

Tammy received a tremendous amount of encouragement in some deep places from her niece's email. It mystified me that people could feel pain for other people's pain, but it was a sweet letter. And I did not think Carrie was in any way crazy; in fact, I was moved: God had spoken to her about us. It hit me that our trial was one small story inside a very big story. God himself had given us Lily. In my heart, a seed was planted.

. . . .

Our agency reiterated to the CCCWA our commitment to Liu Hai Rou. The only reply they got was that they and Civil Affairs both had submitted formal requests for additional checkups, but the orphanage director had not yet sent back the official acceptance forms. That Friday our agency's two highest-ranking in-country staff members spent the entire day on the phone with multiple officials, determined to negotiate something more substantive than more paperwork. They pushed for permission to visit the child. If they could get a picture and some measurements, they said, the family would have concrete information to submit to their own doctor. Even as they spoke, they had a staff member in the provincial capital waiting for their go-ahead. Her name was Joy, and from her hotel room she familiarized herself with Lily's file. Finally, after a day of relentless negotiating, enough pressure had been brought to bear on the orphanage director that at 6PM he acquiesced to a visit the following day.

Word was passed, and Joy prepared to leave. Even though she suffered horribly from motion sickness, for the sake of one sick girl and our family, Joy subjected herself to a five-hour rainy-season bus ride on the high-altitude roads leading to Lily's town. She was allowed to see Lily for mere minutes and learned little of significance. But she became our heroine.

Joy got so sick on the trip back that she was unable to write her report for two days. Once she had, they forwarded us a summary.

> Joy went to the orphanage on Saturday and met Liu Hai Rou in the director's office in the orphanage. Liu Hai Rou was held by her caregiver when she came into the office. She looked like an 8 to 9 month old baby [Lily was fourteen months]. Her hair was thin and yellow. Her lips closed tightly and she held her fists closely and crossed them in front of her chest.
>
> Joy took Hai Rou from her caregiver's hands and held her in her arms. She felt her body was bony and stiff. Joy felt her chest and abdomen and there was almost just skin and bones. Hai Rou turned her head to Joy and saw her face, and then gave Joy a big and happy smile. So Joy saw the child's teeth; she had many teeth already. Her teeth were white and good. She appeared very spirited and bright. Her upper legs were as thin as her calves, there was no muscle on her buttocks.
>
> Hai Rou was put onto the sofa; she was able to sit by herself without any support. Then Joy talked with the director and observed the child's behavior for about ten minutes. During that time, Hai Rou was sitting on the sofa by herself; the caregiver stayed in the office, sitting at the other side of the sofa. Hai Rou began to relax and opened her fist and moved her fingers and arms. She turned her head and moved eyes to look around. She could have eye contact with you and her eyes would follow your movements. During the ten minutes, the baby did not make any noise.
>
> Before the child left the office, Joy and the caregiver tried to help her stand. The caregiver held her arms and let her stretch her legs and let her feet touch the ground, but the child was not able to stand up by the feet.

We read the report all the way through.

Then gasped aloud.

Tammy covered her mouth. A picture.

We barely recognized the little girl staring back at us. Partly from how much time had gone by since the baby pictures we had, but mostly from shock at Lily's thinned and yellowed hair. She was on that sofa, a wooden office sofa in the director's office. Tammy felt sick, suddenly twice as desperate to get her baby out of there. One picture had just made the seriousness of Lily's condition more real to us than all the previous reporting combined.

Recent medical records were attached as well. We dug out our original referral paperwork to compare numbers. To our horror, Lily's weight and height were unchanged. We forwarded everything to a pediatrician in the States and an American doctor living in China. The latter answered first, and finally, eleven days after finding out she was sick, we had some reliable medical input. First, Liu Hai Rou did not have the anemia expected from the reported amount of bleeding, and that sounded encouraging. Further, the doctor contended that her normal red blood cell count strongly argued against serious gastrointestinal bleeding, and therefore her bleeding might only be a side issue.

She had severely low protein stores and electrolyte abnormalities consistent with a history of vomiting. All of these, along with her hair and small size, indicated malnutrition. Her liver showed signs of stress or a possible disorder. But most of the results of her blood test, other than a few results indicating inflammation, possibly in her bone marrow, had come back normal. The doctor felt the root cause of her failure to grow well was not evident by the studies done so far. It was possible repairing her cleft palate would allow some issues to fade away on their own. Or, she could have an underlying inflammatory disease. He wanted to see an HIV test result if available.

He included plenty of scientific terms we had to look up, but we didn't need any help understanding hope, and he had just handed it back to us. Of course taking Lily into our home would involve risk. But we accepted those risks, and it would differ little from having a biological child. They'd not come with any health guarantees; we accepted we had none with her. As we learned more, we wanted her more, not less. We weren't afraid. We were all in. We believed we could nurse her back to health, and the sooner someone let us start doing it, the better.

But those in power did nothing. In fact, the email forwards that came next seemed to imply a consensus was building: our negotiating angles were nearly exhausted. It looked as if the CCCWA might return Liu Hai Rou's file to the orphanage. Maybe soon. We wrote Rebecca for clarification, searching for any strand of hope to cling to. Did any remain?

Rebecca, rather than confirm the worst, surprised us. The Beijing office had come up with one more creative idea for approaching the CCCWA. They said our tenacity had inspired them, and they had made a proposal to bring Liu Hai Rou all the way to Beijing. It would put the entire undertaking and responsibility for her care in the agency's hands. The orphanage would be relieved of custody for an undetermined length of time. The CCCWA could not deny the child had failed to thrive at the orphanage. Everyone rallied around this new idea and hoped that the CCCWA would find it compelling. Beijing did have superior medical facilities. Going there would also provide a more long-term solution than the provincial capital, as our agency had a relationship with a good foster home that could care for Liu Hai Rou for as long as was needed. If only Lily could get there, Beijing sounded perfect.

We immediately gave Rebecca our wholehearted assent, not sure if that was really necessary, but she had been kind enough to ask. Our refusal to give up was making their negotiating position stronger. There was even an initially positive response from the CCCWA.

Unfortunately, word came back that they were going to defer to the orphanage director again before making their decision. Our chances, and our daughter, were still in that man's hands. He'd asked for a day to think it over.

I hoped a direct appeal from us might help sway him. Though I knew nobody important, had no position of strength from which to negotiate, and didn't know what he would find personally persuasive, I poured out our hearts anyway, respecting him as best I could.

Dear Mr. Director,

Thank you for your consideration of this trip to Beijing for Liu Hai Rou. We are very grateful for the care that your orphanage, its leaders, and its caregivers have given her from the time she was a few days old up until now. We are sure that in recent months it has not been easy to care for her when she is so sick. Thank you for persevering and for seeking the best medical care available.

We were very moved by the recent picture of Liu Hai Rou taken in your office, but we are filled with hope that her symptoms may all be reversible with more specialized medical care. We think Beijing is the perfect solution, as there is world-class health care available there. We have personal experience with it. Our son Elijah was born there.

Thank you again, Mr. Director, for your care of our daughter. We have not met her face to face, but we love Liu Hai Rou. We want what is best for her. We believe you do too.

The Johnson Family

Dann, Tammy,

Enoch, Haddie, Elijah, Lily

He gave his permission the following day.

Who said I couldn't negotiate? Consternating indeed not to have picked out a shirt with buttons that morning, so they could have popped off my chest as we read the email.

But then I saw the date stamp. Like a bird sees a picture window. He'd given in the day before I'd written. My chest deflated, and I cradled my pride up off the floor. Adding insult to injury, the agency had tacked on a reminder of the policy that communication from the family is never passed on to anyone.

But no matter. We celebrated just the same. The director had agreed, and Lily would travel to Beijing early the next week. Already the agency was making arrangements to pick up Liu Hai Rou, and drafting the documents that would sign her over into their care. Our exuberance and gratitude were boundless.

Even Rebecca did a victory lap, sending out two short sentences to all involved. We never forgot them: "This girl will get the attention she needs. No matter what the outcome is, she will benefit."

She would benefit. It was very exciting.

Would she be ours? That was still unknown.

The pediatrician's reply came. She was working from the same scant data as the first doctor, but her comments held as much hopeful news as his had. She pointed out that Lily's head was still growing. If the measurements were accurate, this indicated her body was taking in enough nutrients to preserve the brain's development, albeit coming at the expense of the rest of her body. Her head size, however, was extremely small, almost off the chart in only the third percentile. She was in grave condition, but it was less alarming than if her head had stopped growing.

The doctor also felt the data supported the likelihood of learned behavior contributing to the vomiting, in addition to whatever medical reasons were causing it. Gagging herself could have been a habit she developed because eating was causing her pain, from her cleft palate or something else. Her listed allergy to latex, if true, made additional ones, such as food allergies, more likely. Some of her symptoms might be resulting from a twisted bowel. Or, if she truly had been healthy up until the first reports, everything might have been triggered by a change in diet (perhaps from formula to milk), or by parasites, or tuberculosis, or infection.

The doctor had no way of telling if the developmental delays were congenital or from starving and then the resultant loss of muscle mass. It was impossible to say whether or not the sickness's effects would be reversible. They might be permanent. Or they might disappear with nutrition and therapy. The doctor emphasized the gravity of her immediate condition, while at the same time commiserating with us. She knew all the decisions were out of our hands. Her final conclusion: "Diet changes, checking for allergies, or looking for and treating infections may save her."

Hopeful yet dire.

More than ever, we were anxious to see Lily out of her orphanage and in Beijing. They had said "early next week," so we hoped to hear news about the transfer by Tuesday or Wednesday. Tuesday was the earliest in any week that we got news, as all communication was routed through agency headquarters in the U.S. and lost a day to time changes before coming back to us in China. When Wednesday night came and still no news, we were on tenterhooks. The waiting of past months had not immunized us to its chafing now.

What is the delay? Do we stay up late hoping for a U.S. morning email, or do we go to bed so we can get up before the U.S. workday ends?

We stayed up late. And woke up early.

Any time Rebecca phoned, it was just before she left the office —our early morning—but no call came on Thursday morning. So we checked email for the third hopeful morning in a row…nothing.

All of Thursday dragged by.

On Friday we finally got a call. Rebecca had news, but it wasn't good. The orphanage director had not signed the written documents, effectively nullifying his own verbal permission. We hung up stunned.

A second long weekend lasting until Tuesday loomed. The stress of not knowing became a weight almost heavier than even final bad news would be. How long can the human heart endure equal doses of hope and disappointment?

The weekend finally terminated with a Tuesday morning email more frustrating than getting nothing at all would have been— some banal report about a switch to soy formula that had been made days earlier and had no effect. The vomiting went on. Though no blood of late. Intravenous drips every day. We read through to the end; the transfer failed to get even a mention.

Confirmation that Lily could go to Beijing was an impotent promise grown stale. The debate over her fate raged on. Somewhere else. Out of our sight and void of our input.

Uncertainty reigned, and was taking its toll.

We were worn to a nub.

News had to come soon.

Fighting for Her Life

*Is there a peculiar love given us
for those that God wills to take from us?*

Harriet Beecher Stowe

IT DID.

ON THURSDAY, Rebecca sent this:

> Dear Dann and Tammy:
> Here is the e-mail describing the situation. Please know how very
> sorry I am.
> Take care,
> Rebecca Makos

> Hello Rebecca,
> Director Liu of the CCCWA had a phone call conversation with
> [our Director] Silvia this morning to clarify their final opinion on
> the case of Liu Hai Rou:
> After discussion with the orphanage and the provincial Civil
> Affairs office and the careful consideration, the CCCWA would
> like to withdraw Liu Hai Rou's match. The CCCWA suggested
> the family to decline Liu Hai Rou and they would help with the
> family's new match. The CCCWA much appreciated everything
> our family did for the child, and meanwhile they were very sorry
> for the unexpected result. On behalf of adoptive families, the
> CCCWA could not match any child with a lot of unknown
> health problems; on behalf of adopted children, they could not
> keep continuing arranging the family's coming waiting for the

child's health status. Considering of all mentioned above, the CCCWA would like to stop moving on her adoption process.

Silvia requested that since our family has already returned back the LOA, could they hold on to the match with Liu Hai Rou and wait for her further medical evaluation and treatment, while the agency could oversee all the medicals and cover the fees. But Director Liu did not accept our requests. The relevant departments preferred the medical process to be separated from the adoption procedure.

Take care,

Ivy

Disbelief washed over us. It was ending. They were ending it.

Tammy wept quietly.

I stared.

Being accosted twice by the tired English sign-off "take care" was salt in the wound of being told that we couldn't. All we wanted to do was take care of Lily. But no, we would not be taking care of her, ever. I struggled to take it in. Really and truly, they weren't going to let us have her. Regardless of the advantages a family offered over an orphanage and a foster home, in spite of our willingness to wait for further diagnoses and postpone our pickup, other factors were obviously more important. There was policy, there was precedent. Power and procedure. Relationships. Face. We had no idea what the deal breakers were.

We were too naive to make any sense of the orphanage director's delays and refusal to approve further care. A child so obviously and desperately in need of intervention could have been helped almost immediately after her sickness became known outside the orphanage. But weeks had passed, and nothing had changed.

Much more time would pass before we could piece together theories of what he must have been thinking. In essence, he needed her to stay sick. If she went off somewhere and began to recover, she'd stay matched with us. But then his name and his blunders with the match would remain a part of her record. Far better to quietly close the door on his handling of Liu Hai Rou's illness. Get the file back. Eliminate her connection with anyone outside the orphanage. Start over. Should she happen to live.

We will never know all the particulars—promotion, demotion, face, discipline—affecting his decisions, nor what exactly it was he valued protecting, but it wasn't a sick little girl. He had demanded the return of her file, and he wasn't going to release her until he had it. Our attachment to Lily was what stood in his way, so she became his bargaining chip.

For everyone else, the girl's sickness had been a medical emergency.

For him, it had been just the leverage he needed.

We spent the better part of an hour in semi-shock on the phone with Rebecca, her sentiments barely registering, replies dying on our lips.

We had not been off the phone long when something happened to me. Inside me. A transition, as if from sleep to wake, reorienting me. I'd been sitting on our maroon sofa chair by the corner window in our living room when it came: I had to fight for her. I was Lily's dad. Had not God given her to me? I had a role. Imminent loss awakened me to action. Heightened feelings of love came over me, and I no longer cared if others thought me crazy. I did not care how naive I might be. We were not taking no for an answer. Not without a fight. Besides, if we had learned anything from living in China, it was that everything, even the non-negotiable, is negotiable. Lily needed me. I was going to fight for her.

I may not have been a memorable negotiator, but I was no stranger to arguing. I sat down to compose a letter. Not exactly the most fearsome form of attack in the history of human conflict, in spite of axioms about pens being mightier than swords. But those pens made history because the right people read what they wrote. Who would read this letter? I would be writing CCCWA Director Liu himself. What to say and how to say it were already filling my mind. I was positive that a passable Chinese letter could do more good than a brilliant English one, even if the director understood English. But it would mean leaving things out because I lacked the language to say them. My trepidation over beginning was overcome by a building sense of urgency. And (I noted with some surprise) rage. Liu Hai Rou was powerless to defend herself. I would not stand by while others made decisions about her life and ours without at least shouting that I didn't like it.

I wrestled with my five-year old Mandarin for five hours until I felt I'd coaxed out as much as I could. Besides, I had to quit sometime. I included a postscript informing the director that the agency office had our phone numbers, and a second apologizing for any inappropriateness, laying the blame at the feet of my limited Chinese, both culture and language. The body of the letter translates[14]

62

as follows:

> Dear Director Liu,
>
> Hello, my name is Dann Johnson, and were we to meet, you could use my Chinese name, Zhan Di En. You can tell that's a transliteration. Chinese colleagues chose that name for me eleven years ago, long before I spoke any Chinese myself. I truly hope that this letter is passed on and you are now reading it for yourself.
>
> Let me begin by saying thank you so much for your care, for your support. We would have never heard of Liu Hai Rou were it not for the CCCWA, never would have gotten her picture, never would have come to feel in our hearts that she is our daughter. So thank you.
>
> But we are heartbroken.
>
> First, let me say that I understand the reasons for your decision. I understand that Lily Anne (that's her new English name) has been in poor health for months. I understand that the last few weeks of the process have been far from normal.
>
> But three times before I have felt the love that a father has for his own child. Lily Anne is my fourth. Each one of these four is special. Were I to lose any of my other three, could I ever say, "Well, that's that, let's just have another"? No one would even suggest such a thing. Yet we are feeling about Lily what we would feel about our current children. I know that legally we have yet to be declared Lily's parents, but our hearts say different.
>
> When we heard of the decision to take Lily Anne to Beijing, we were excited. We were even more encouraged by the updated medical and lab results—perhaps her sickness was not as bad as we had feared.
>
> Director Liu, we hope that you are able to understand our hearts, and why we had to write you this letter. We respect you, and we will abide by your final decision.
>
> But we are pleading with you to reconsider.
>
> We love Lily Anne.
>
> When we started the adoption process last year, we had no specific orphan that we had met and wanted to adopt. But it's not like that anymore. We know Lily. She has entered our family. Everyone calls her "old four."[15] Not a day goes by that her brothers and sister do not say her name. Her two-year-old broth-

er says "Meimei de" ["little sister's"] every time he touches her crib, or pushes her stroller, or picks up her little clothes.

We know this situation is complicated. We know how many people have been supportive and want to see Lily Anne healthy again. Once more, thank you. But you must know how willing we are to be patient. We can wait if it means that bringing Lily home might still be possible.

We hope you can accept our proposal and might very soon give us good news, because at the moment our hearts, and I speak especially on behalf of my wife's, are truly broken.

Sincerely,
Dann Johnson
and Tammy Johnson

We had to rush. A holiday break was starting, and we were desperate to get the letter into the Director's hands before offices closed. I daydreamed about getting on a plane and pressing it into his hands myself.

I knew that directly writing the Beijing staff would put me on shaky ground with the home office. Throughout the nightmare they had been generous and unorthodox in their openness by giving us access to in-house communication. I did not want to be taking unfair advantage of that. Regarding writing the director himself, there was no vagueness in policy. It wasn't allowed. But I felt confident our case was so unusual that the agency would make an exception. I believed their ultimate desire was the same as ours: the preservation of the match. Regardless, my decision was made. This was the only way of fighting I had.

For the first time ever, I emailed Beijing. I explained to Ivy what I wanted, and I promised her I was not trying to undermine authority or flaunt policy or ask her to break rules. But sending our letter directly to her was the only way of getting it to the director before the holiday. I copied Rebecca on the email, but waiting for her permission would have meant a four-day delay. Four days was an eternity. I pleaded with Ivy to deliver the letter—it would mean so much to us.

Within the hour Ivy wrote back with the crushing news that our letter could not be given because the CCCWA had been closed early for the holiday that whole day, anyway. But she could not have delivered it without Rebecca's permission, either. It was a moot point, now. We'd failed.

We were almost frantic thinking about what the next four days might be like. I couldn't help writing Ivy back immediately. I told her that, though dispirited, we understood her need to speak to Rebecca. But the rest of my words basically only pulled back the thin veil covering our desperation: "perhaps you could call the director's mobile just to let him know there is a letter"; or "if you only knew how much peace we would find in just knowing that he knew we'd written." Embarrassing stuff. But my sole thought was to fight for Lily, and if there had been other words to think of, I would doubtlessly have embarrassed myself further. Again I copied Rebecca and again I apologized if I was over the line.

The holiday weekend dragged by. We had limitless time for agonizing over the letter into which I had poured our hopes, and this only fed our wild hopes about how it might be received.

But they were misplaced. In the end, the letter was given to no one.

> Any contact with the CCCWA is absolutely prohibited. As the CCCWA has told us that the adoption process must stop before we can get involved with the child's medical assistance, we do not feel your letter should be submitted, nor would it help your situation at all, and would likely hurt your situation.
> We will let you know if there are any developments. The CC-CWA has assured us they will help you with a re-match.
> We know your hearts are broken with this development. But you have already helped this child immensely. We will be working with the Beijing office to make sure your letter is properly handled.

In other words, shredded.

I felt stupid and shamed. In everyone's minds, then, it was over. They were the professionals, telling us how things were; we were the hysterical parents, screaming soundlessly.

But I would not accept defeat so easily. I had determined to fight, and it would be no fight if we rolled over this quickly. So what that the agency had no say in the matter? So what that they weren't calling the shots? That didn't mean we had to stand by silently, too. I would not accept that our commitment, our willingness to wait, and our love were of no consequence. I refused to believe they were incapable of affecting the situation.

We prayed for a change in someone's heart; we prayed for a

change in circumstances. Anything that would cause our letter to be given to Director Liu and renew hope that our love for this child might still bring her to us. I poured out my thoughts in emails. Maybe the agency could not support our fight for her, but I demanded to know if they acknowledged the logic of our position, and could at least sympathize with that. But I demeaned myself more than I knew as I nursed an insatiable need for process satisfaction along with proof that at the very least we were being heard. Didn't us living in-country count for anything? We didn't need to coordinate between two governments, we could do the Chinese side of the adoption immediately. What about our language ability? I possessed some measure of expertise on cultural appropriateness, and wouldn't go charging in loudly like some clueless American. Why couldn't we go to her? Did none of these factors matter?

At no point, I vigorously clarified, were we ever hoping to "help Lily Anne immensely." That may have been good news to everyone else, but it was borderline offensive to us. Our hope had been to bring our daughter home. That alone was the kind of help we'd signed up to give. Understandably, they could rejoice an orphan was being helped. We were losing a family member.

I said many things, some more embarrassing than others when I read everything back later. Most of it read like arguing, but it was all sent because we were convinced we deserved an audience with the director. It was our only plea. We had nothing else.

Maybe something I said would sway our agency at the last minute. Maybe there would be an eleventh-hour reversal from the CCCWA. Maybe we would get a miracle.

Hope dies hard.

We asked Rebecca to share any ultimate bad news via email, and for goodness' sake not to call and force us to talk about it on the phone again.

Yet die it must.

The final blow came rolled up in enough past tense to heap scorn on me for ever having believed there was second-chance hope. We'd been fools. The rescinding had been irrevocable the moment it was spoken. Medical treatment was contingent on dissolution of the match—that was the ultimatum. And at that moment we'd lost the advocacy of our own agency. In spite of my anguish over how to best fight, there had never been a single thing I could have done to make a difference. No words, at any time, in either language, could have changed anything.

The attitude of CCCWA is very clear: all medical treatment for this child could not continue as long as you were matched with her. The CCCWA will not consider continuing with this match. This is their final decision.

Please know that this child will be helped and has already been helped due to your determination, persistence, and faith in her. We will be continuing to help her, and that is good news.

Please let me know when you feel up to talking this through, and when you feel ready to consider another child.

It was over. Truly.

I had shouted my displeasure. I might as well have whispered to a whirlwind. The decision was final. Further persistence was unwelcome. We were out of people who would fight for us, and we were out of people to fight with. It was too soon to feel any comfort from knowing Lily was going to be helped. She was gone.

There was no longer anyone to fight for.

How does the heart recover from yearning for a miracle destined never to arrive? Our yearning had lasted for thirty-three days. Our miracle wasn't coming. I dazedly sought out the corner chair where I'd decided to fight for her and collapsed into it, my insides on an uncharted free fall. I helplessly watched a blurry living room Lily would never play in.

This is grief? It feels like this? For everyone? I've lived this long and have never known this? People everywhere have always felt like THIS *when they lose someone they love? It hurts* THIS *much? How can it hurt this much? What is she doing right now? How long can it possibly hurt this much?*

The day did end. So did the next, and the one after that.

I'd watched weeping people bereft of loved ones before, but I'd never felt their losses. I'd had no capacity to, because I hadn't known loss myself. Now Loss and Pain had come to my door. There was shock in how painful the pain was, but at the same time it also hit home: I *could* hurt. I was a regular human being. I had the distinct feeling I was joining the rest of humanity in a way I'd never known I never had.

. . . .

Three days passed before we managed to share our Lily news. I

67

made a brief attempt at putting words to our feelings, only to delete every draft. In the end we sent a short statement confirming that Lily's adoption was over. The email was signed, "Dann, Tammy, Enoch, Haddie, Elijah, but no Lily."

Many wrote back, some beautifully.[16]

A few said things we'd have rather been left unsaid, and I wondered how many times I had spoken to others who were in pain when silence would have been more healing. We marveled at the letters from people who had lost children. We had not expected such a connection to them, as we'd never even seen Lily. But without exception, these people understood our loss, and that gave us a freedom and permission to fully grieve it. This was death, and we were justified in feeling it. To us, Lily was dying. Whether she recovered or not, she was not joining our family. The dream was dead. Lily Anne Johnson did not exist.

Tammy journaled:

> Dear Lord,
> Today the Door Closed. Lily is no longer ours. But she is still Yours. May she be loved, be a part of a family, though it cannot be ours. Your path for her is somewhere else.
> So many people have been praying for her. I know You are with her. But there still is so much I do not understand. But I will trust. I know You will use this for her good and for ours.
> Help us let go. Help us open our hearts equally to another child.
> If I would be able to talk to Lily someday I would want to say, "Lily, when you were just a small sick baby, you were dearly loved. You had a family who loved you and waited to bring you home. But our paths only crossed briefly and did not join. Yet in that crossing we changed one another's lives. Loving you has taught us a deeper meaning of love, to love when it hurts, to love even when the one you love does not know, to fight for that love, to lose and to hurt and yet trust God.
> And we have brought you the attention you needed to be better cared for.
> We pray that you will be taken to a doctor, that you will be healed, and that you will never again be neglected. You are loved by us, by our friends, and by our Heavenly Father. We pray you will know a family who loves you, that you will Belong, be Beloved, and grow up to be like a Lily among thorns. As we see your eyes shine in your picture even though sick, may your heart

equally shine one day with God's love, your health be touched by His hand, and your head be filled with His wisdom and knowledge. Even though our paths may never cross again, they did for four months and for those four months you were our Lily. We love you and miss you. We grieve losing you, for you were our child and it seemed so real. We now hand you over to our loving Father who will watch over and care for you better than we can. So many have prayed for you.

Goodbye, Lily Anne. Goodbye Liu Hai Rou. We love you!

Give them all, give them all, give them all to Jesus, and he will turn your sorrow into joy.[17]

The only place Tammy was wrong was in thinking our paths would never cross again.

Reeling Silk

病来如山倒，病去如抽丝

*Sickness comes like an avalanche,
but goes like reeling silk.*

Chinese saying

TO SAY THAT THE CCCWA assisted us with a rematch would have been an understatement. We had a new referral in hand even before breaking our news about losing Lily. Including transoceanic relays, it had taken two days. Which meant (I realized later with some distaste) the new girl had been in place before Lily was taken from us. It felt surreal to be given so quickly something for which people usually waited months and years.

Ding Jing Feng, our new match, was four months older than Liu Hai Rou. She, too, had a cleft soft palate. And she lived right down the road. Astonishing evidence that the long arm of the CCCWA was indeed being extended in our favor. We'd have to travel less than an hour to pick her up—clearly they wanted us pleased. Or placated. We would rather have been celebrating the use of their power to give us Lily, but we told ourselves that such wishing was counterproductive now. We were not angry at the CCCWA, but neither did the special attention feel personally meaningful.

I found there was something that did make me angry: looking at Ding Jing Feng.

The poor child, I couldn't help it.

Tammy thought her precious, and stared long and deeply into

her sad eyes, wondering if they were the eyes of her new daughter. I saw a stranger. A stranger I didn't want to know.

You are most definitely not my daughter! I know what my daughter looks like. How could I love you? You are not her.

Over the next hours we went back to the computer again and again to look at her mournful face. It brooded back at me from the arms of an elderly auntie, defying me to love her. I obliged.

I won't love you. I don't want to love you. I don't want you at all. I only want....

I was light years from wanting this referral. We had told our agency we would be ready, but we were wrong. I never dreamt they could mean two days.

Tammy was raw over Lily too, but compassion made it impossible for her to dismiss Ding Jing Feng out of hand. She couldn't quickly reject any child she'd contemplated as daughter, even for a moment. She also cringed to wonder if rejecting Ding Jing Feng could somehow derail her file from being quickly referred to another family.

Which made me think of something else to worry about. Not Ding Jing Feng's file, but our own. What if we point-blank rebuffed the CCCWA's obvious favor? Could we damage ourselves? Would it be somehow failing to give them face? Knowing the eminent importance of face in Asian culture had done very little to make me an expert about what exactly it was in real life that gave face, or caused its loss. Rebecca put my worries to rest. She assured us we had nothing to fear, and the CCCWA had already told her that acceptance of the Ding Jing Feng match was voluntary. If it was too soon for us, we were genuinely free to turn it down.

So Tammy and I continued to discuss it, but I was never close. In the end we agreed to decline. Ding Jing Feng belonged in another family. And it would be so much better if first memories of our new daughter, whoever she was going to be, were happy ones for both of us.

Ding Jing Feng receded from our lives as quickly as she'd come. In the months following, I often found Tammy staring at her six pictures, crying and wondering what would happen to her. One little girl among millions, she was special because for one brief moment she'd held the potential to become ours. Tammy prayed for her to be united with her forever family soon, and that they would love Jesus, and raise her to know the unconditional affection and love of her Heavenly Father.

71

For my part, the requirements of discussing Ding Jing Feng and her file had done me good. It forced me to recognize that our adoption roller coaster was still hurtling forward. I had to move beyond Lily. Grief's stages yet seeped through me, but I herded my heart toward being ready to receive a daughter that would not be her.

Only to be jerked on a sudden dive in the opposite direction.

Lily's health turned a corner.

While on the phone with the Beijing office, a staff member happened to mention it. My heart stuttered, then I did as asked her to explain.

Liu Hai Rou had been sent to Beijing immediately after being unmatched with us. Her orphanage director had signed all the papers and was no longer involved. Lily was living at the Beijing foster home we'd been told about. Some time after getting there, she had begun to keep food down. She was no longer starving.

"Diagnosis?"

No diagnosis, just better.

"How much better?"

Tammy and I took deep breaths and finished one another's sentences about remaining guarded. Our hope the first time had been so fervent, then so devastated. The mere thought of a repeat was paralysis. We refused our hearts the license to hope. We dashed off an inquiry about the possibilities of putting new matches on hold so we could monitor Liu Hai Rou's improvements, but we were tentative. Our curiosity was piqued, but the sting of their prior rebuff was fresh enough to permit me only hints at our deepest questions. Enough courage apparently remained for a whiff of it to sneak into my last sentence: "We would have come for her when she was at her sickest, and we would come for her now."

Our agency's response floored us. They made no promises, and could say nothing of time frames, but they were amenable to the possibility of opening a negotiation with the CCCWA about a rematch. The first thing they needed to know was how long we were willing to wait. Three weeks prior, that question would have been a no-brainer: "As long as it takes."

Now it wasn't so simple. We'd grieved a lot in three weeks. What if we waited again, only to have it end the same way again? We were under no delusions now that we could affect the process positively just because we loved her. On the other hand, three weeks was nothing in comparison to who Lily had been to us. And now she was perhaps being offered back to us? Back on the first hand, however, the effects of processing three weeks of grief were undeniable. We'd made every effort to force ourselves to move on, consider the next child, and acknowledge that we had a dossier full of time-sensitive documents that would not remain valid forever.

We could give no answer. We needed more information. We didn't dare bend toward hope if it would only mean getting our teeth kicked in. What factors would be driving the decision about when to rematch her? Was a diagnosis going to be required before moving forward? What if there never was one? How long would the CCCWA require she remain healthy without relapse?

When we hung up the phone with Rebecca, I headed to the airport. In an odd turn of events, a high-level director from our agency was coming to visit us. We'd never had any dealings with her before, but she was in the country on business and had, of her own volition and to our great surprise, volunteered to rework her itinerary and do our home study update. It was a brief but required addendum that our new permanent address in China necessitated. There were few social workers available in China with the proper credentials to do such updates, so her generosity benefitted us greatly. After our interviews, she had even happier news. She had arranged for the agency to meet for negotiations with several CCCWA directors.

We tried not to get excited about such high-level chess moves being executed on our behalf, but it was hard not to. Liu Hai Rou was due for a doctor's appointment that Saturday, and negotiations would be convened directly afterwards. We took deep breaths all through the weekend.

On Tuesday morning Rebecca called.

The CCCWA's answer, in no uncertain terms, was no.

This time we rolled over without a fight, for there was no fight in us. We let go once more.

Not a day went by that we didn't think of Lily and pray for Lily. Eventually we gained enough distance to see the silver lining in our four-month connection. She wasn't out of the woods yet, but we learned she hadn't thrown up since arriving in Beijing. She was beginning to put on weight. Solely because she had been matched with us, she had been snatched from a likely fatal situation and placed on the road to recovery. We didn't know anything about the people who now cared for her, or why they had been chosen, or if we would ever know, but we were thankful for them. They would always be the people who took care of the girl who was supposed to have been our daughter.

It was time to move on to the girl who really would be.

And so that fall we transitioned from grief to waiting again, the final time before our first adoption journey would come to a close and culminate in the Christmas present we named Eden. But first, one of the busiest seasons we'd ever known engulfed us at work, and we welcomed the distraction from our pain. Time and again our hearts were pushed aside by minds occupied with the tyranny of busyness.

We had moved back to Xi'an to open a culture center. The ancient capital city of Xi'an, home to the Terracotta Army and many other historical sites left over from the ten dynasties who governed there over the centuries, had been our first China home. We loved Xi'an, and still had friends there from our years during language school at Shaanxi Normal University. Now we were returning for this entrepreneurial venture. The culture center needed to get off the ground and open for business before year's end. Downstairs would house a coffee shop; upstairs would have office space and rooms for kids clubs, adult English modules, preschool, and tutoring. Most of these programs would eventually offer programming in both English and Chinese.

That fall was about creating the facility. It was a tremendous challenge for a pack of greenhorn foreigners, especially when it came to navigating the maze of official permissions needed at every stage: the city government, the district government, the fire department, the management office, the sanitation department, the health department, the keeping up appearances department. China was developing at a dizzying pace, and straight answers could be hard to come by. Regulations written in the more-developed east did not always have a one-to-one correlation to reality in our city. We struggled to differentiate between which edicts were negotiable and which weren't. And which ones didn't even exist, but had been pulled out of some official's hat merely for personal benefit. While we foreigners worked hard at understanding the importance of relationships in China, we would have been utterly lost without our local staff. Together we challenged ourselves to procure everything we needed by means other than bribing. We didn't always know how to best grease the wheels, but we did learn we could earn more favor with respect than without it, and that showing up in Santa hats and reindeer antlers to deliver Christmas cookies and provide a few photo ops with the silly foreigners got better results than any amount of arguing we'd ever done. We made plenty of gaffes along the way, and I was grateful every day I didn't shoot myself in the cultural foot.

My job was designing everything from the floor plan to the fire door route maps[18] to the location of outlets. The first floor needed a kitchen and a restroom. The second floor needed classrooms, storage, a restroom, and office space. A friend recommended two workmen who had built some shelving for her, and they turned out to be a goldmine. We hired them for the whole project, and they sub-contracted the jobs they couldn't or didn't want to do themselves. I oversaw them and they oversaw everyone else.

Our inaugural project was hanging a new floor in the open stairwell, creating floor space out of the air for a bathroom and a storage room. Then came decisions about where to run water lines, where to run all the electric wiring (routed in channels chipped out of the concrete with impact drills), where to put lights, how many and what kind of lights for each space in the building, where to locate closets, how large to make the classrooms, which type and what quality of building materials to choose for the walls, for the ceilings, for the flooring...the decisions were endless. They came at me in such numbers I had a hard time turning off my mind at night and going to sleep. Pain over Lily was pushed aside. The day came when some word or thought could jolt my mind to her and I would realize with surprise it was the first time I'd thought of her that day.

The two workers and I did everything together. I accompanied them on every supply run, bantered with them over every decision. Sometimes I asked them to do things in a way they'd never seen it done before, but I wouldn't bend. Other times I would have been a fool not to bow to their superior expertise. I learned when to be stubborn, and they learned how to convince me that's all I was being. Once in a great while we might have gotten on each other's nerves, but mostly we laughed a lot. And worked hard. They had the same surname but weren't related. Master Wang and Master Wang, I only ever called them Pair of Wangs. Their camaraderie was a balm to my sad soul while I healed from Lily.

Toward Health

Of course, in a novel, people's hearts break, and they die, and that is the end of it; and in a story this is very convenient. But in real life we do not die when all that makes life bright dies to us.
There is a most busy and important round of eating, drinking, dressing, walking, visiting, buying, selling, talking, reading, and all that makes up what is commonly called LIVING, yet to be gone through.

Harriet Beecher Stowe

TAMMY AND I BOTH healed.

And went back to waiting. Tammy asked the agency about Ding Jing Feng, hoping to put her concern to rest for good, and she did. Ding Jing Feng had been matched with a family. Our family was ready for a match, too, but no referrals materialized in our agency's batch of matchable children that month. So our wait would be stretched at least another month, meaning no happy medium between two days and two months. We felt impatient again, eager to finish what we had set out to do: welcome a parentless child into our home.

We loved the beautiful Old Testament name *Eden*. Enoch and Haddie were gradually transferring their affections to this new sister, though losing Lily had impacted them, too. Now they prayed for both girls, and not just for Lily to get better, but to get a family. Poor two-year-old Elijah was having none of it. "No!" he shouted one night, funnily still with his ever-present smile, correcting us about whose crib was in Haddie's room: "That's Lily Anne's!" He wasn't going to stand for any trespass from this Eden interloper, whoever she was.

As construction in the culture center wound down, life slowed again, and we had time to wonder what she'd be like. Where she'd be from. Excitement built, but it would never reach Lily levels. Hurt did not allow our hearts to go that far.

At least we could rest assured that our hearts were in good physical shape: we'd had them checked. Health checks are a non-stop part of life in China. Health check for a visa, health check for a residence permit, and now a brand new one for opening a restaurant. The biggest difference between these health checks and ones we might get at home is the sheer number of personnel involved. This was no visit to one doctor assisted by one nurse; it was a station check. One doctor checked your eyes, wrote on your form, and sent you on down the hall where you'd get your blood pressure checked. Or your chest X-ray. Blood samples, urine samples, ear checks, everything had its own room. Once you understood how it worked, it was fairly slick. You didn't even have to do the steps in order, just find the room with the shortest line at the door and make sure you didn't leave any space between yourself and the person in front of you.

The test that got foreigners talking the most was the ECG. I'd been told this was the same test of the body's electrical system that TV-hero Johnny Gage[19] from my childhood would have referred to as an EKG, but they didn't look anything alike to me. The ECG never failed to elicit a little mirth from us foreigners. You lay back on a cot in a cubicle, pulled up one pant leg and your shirt front—along with any other torso garments regardless of gender—up to your neck, and didn't move. The doctor slathered cold gel (that brought some of the laughs right there) on your chest and ankle, attached a number of clamps that I would be comfortable using as jumper cables in a pinch, then inspected the resulting electrical data on a screen. Tammy always had the additional excitement of the race between the doctor yelling "someone's in here!" and next-guy-in-line popping his head over the cubicle barrier to ask if it was his turn yet. In the test you couldn't feel anything but the cold gel, but it was still always nice to say, "That's done for another year."

The health check specifically for restaurant workers contained one test we'd never seen before. They separated the men and the women. Our group's six women—three foreigners and three national staff—went into one room along with two strangers swept in at the same time. I would soon have reason to be glad my room held only me and our one male staff member. The doctor handed us each a cotton swab. My eyes widened as I heard his instructions. My coworker, mistaking slack-jaw for lack of comprehension, provided me with a loose translation: "Get some waste!"

It was quite simple, actually, to loosen our buckles, reach in, and swab out. Once there was enough color to satisfy the doctor, we were done. The system did not even require an entire petri dish for my small sample. Instead, each dish had been neatly segmented with a permanent marker into eight equal pie shapes. My swab got wiped into space number five, and that same number along with the petri dish number were written down on my form. Why waste eight petri dishes for eight samples when one will do? I actually found the methodology preferable to the jars, lids, sticks, and plastic wrap over a toilet that our American doctor's tests had prescribed.

Next door we could hear they were having a rollicking time. Like us, the ladies had had no idea what the test was when they entered. The eight of them were herded into a circle still wearing their winter coats, facing one another. The female doctor commanded, "Drop your pants." Which they proceeded to do, but not without an escaped snort from one of the Americans. Cotton swabs were passed around. At the instructions someone else giggled, and once the foreigners got going, our local staff couldn't stop, either. Even the two strangers joined in, whether from the contagion of being with loopy people or simply at them, nobody knew. Once all tests were finished and we were together on the street again, the girls were still laughing so hard we couldn't understand what they were trying to tell us. We'd driven for blocks before they could paint a clear picture of their story, by which time it was too late to tell them that maybe we didn't need one.

That week we finished painting the coffee shop ceiling, and I carelessly referred to the color as "Q-tip brown." It stuck.

. . . .

As expected, our referral came the next month.

We pored over the four pictures of our new daughter. In one especially, I thought Eden resembled a peanut, and it's been my favorite ever since. The paperwork listed her date of birth as that very day. Our joy at the match was tinged with disappointment as once again we missed a first birthday with a daughter-to-be. It moved us to begin praying we'd get her by Christmas, in spite of the long odds.

My Beijing trip came. The freshly signed LOA that I would hand-deliver there would be Eden's, not Lily's. New child, new LOA. Other than the one bit of news about Lily doing better, we'd heard nothing further. It hadn't seemed appropriate to keep nagging for information. But while arranging the trip to Beijing, I could no longer resist.

The home office had told me to communicate about the LOA drop off directly with Director Sylvia, whom I only knew by name. When she personally replied to my email asking about Liu Hai Rou, my heart jumped: Lily's improvement had never stopped. In fact, her health was quite good. Ivy had gone to visit her the week before and had taken pictures and videos. I would be welcome to see them. I wrote back that I would love that, then wrote and rewrote my closing sentence a dozen times, seeking just the right wording to achieve a tone that would have Sylvia believing I was in earnest yet avoid making me sound desperate. Or creepy or crazy or even pesky—we did still have an adoption in process. I settled on simple. "We would adopt both girls in a heartbeat if anyone would let us."

I couldn't get it out of my head that the right word at the right time to the right person might still work a miracle. The slimmest of possibilities would expand in my imagination like Amish friendship bread at high altitude. The tiniest cracks of opportunity inside my mind erupted into wide doorways. The one called *Lily* had its door still shut just the same, but how could I not lean on it to see what happened?

What if it is still possible, even now, to have the whole Lily chapter reduced to a bad dream?

Sylvia didn't reply.

I couldn't stop thinking about what she might say in person. When a few days later I walked into her office, I was still thinking about it. There were smiles all around while I passed out the local Xi'an snacks I'd brought. I also had one wrapped gift for Joy. "Would you please forward this to her office and personally thank her for us one more time?" They promised they would.

I felt the air thick with my unanswered inquiry, so when the other staff had gone back to their desks, I repeated myself. "Sylvia, I'm serious. We would take both girls, we truly would." Her reply was tactful, even kind, but made me feel it was best not to push any harder. It would be unfair, she said, for one family to be given two while hundreds of others waited for one. Logical. She said a little bit more, neither more nor less than what she should have said, and I knew I was listening to the limits of Sylvia's authority, not of her kindness. But I was disappointed all the same. They were words of policy spoken by a professional. Every orphan precious and equal. Exactly what one would expect and desire from an adoption professional. But I was not a professional. And "fairness" was the reason I could not have Lily? Nothing, ever, had felt more unfair than that.

It was only a few weeks later that we were making our trip down to Guangzhou. Grandparents had long planned to share that Christmas with us, and so it worked perfectly to have them still there to watch three of their grandchildren while we traveled to get one more. We left a few days after Christmas and the girl we met on those red, white, and black couches was Eden, not Lily.

The first twenty-four hours are officially labeled the trial period, and families are given the right during those twenty-four hours to change their minds and decline to take their matched child home. Mind-blowingly, even at that late juncture, a few do. Fortunately for us, it was not a right that extended both ways.[20] We sent a joking email to friends the next day:

> We've discovered, not surprisingly, that Eden is not the cry-proof angel we wrote about yesterday. In fact, she often screams out of panicked fear, and her non-reaction to us yesterday is now puzzling. Perhaps she was in a daze from her long bus trip. Or drugged. She has latched on to Tammy, and somehow even said *Mama* on the first day, and continues to do so. If anything, her desire to be with Tammy has only grown in the 30 hours we have been together, which is a good thing. A host of things can be counted on to make her scream, but the top five boil down to these:
> 1. Dann holding her.
> 2. Dann looking at her.
> 3. Dann moving between her and Tammy.
> 4. Dann feeding her.
> 5. Dann.
> Tammy is exhausted. She didn't get much sleep with a sweaty little girl's body mashed on top of her face all night.

We signed the papers on the following day and were cleared to return home the day after that. While hanging out in a coffee shop near the White Swan our last evening, we met a family who, like us, had lost their match. It was startling to encounter people who could so closely relate to our Lily story. Sitting in their laps was just-adopted Katie. But Katie wasn't Katie. The girl they loved, the girl they'd first named Katie, the girl they had flown across the ocean to pick up, was not the girl they had been given upon arrival. There hadn't even been time to choose another name. As to what had happened to first Katie, other than the sketchiest of details, they mainly had guesses. Shock etched their every expression, struggle and joy over the second girl side by side with their grief for the first.[21]

Even in the worst that life had thrown at me, I had something to be thankful for. We had gotten to experience grief and joy months apart, not minutes apart. We knew where our lost daughter was, and at least some details about what had happened to her. In a totally foreign experience for me, my heart ached, literally hurt, for these people. Nothing like that had ever happened to me before Lily.

We flew home with Eden just in time to ring in the New Year as a family of six, a fortuitous number in China. Counting grandparents made eight, the most fortuitous number of all. It was thrilling to finally have our daughter home, and we enjoyed a few days of ignorant bliss before reality struck. With every month that passed, we thought of Lily less.

Fabulously Harebrained

Risk comes from not knowing what you're doing.

Warren Buffett

WE KNEW LILY WAS on the road to health, but we didn't know how long we would be able to keep track of where she went. When she fully recovered, she would be returned to her orphanage and matched again. Did our agency's oversight of her current care mean they would get her file again when the time came? We didn't know. If the file went to another agency, she could be matched with a family from anywhere. Maybe she would grow up speaking Dutch. Or Norwegian. We hated the thought of never learning her fate, never finding out if she had been adopted at all. But continuing to wear out our welcome with constant inquiries to the agency was also distasteful.

Meanwhile, the timeline named *Eden* scraped itself forward across our lives.

Then paperwork trouble reared up out of nowhere again.

Once upon an unsophisticated time, I'd thought paperwork ended completely with the dossier, but nothing could be further from the truth, especially for expatriate families. A month after we'd weathered the three months of the worst screaming, we had to get to U.S. soil. It was time for our citizenship run. For most Americans, their adoptive child's citizenship resulted automatically when the child naturalized upon arrival on U.S. soil, and a process began that would culminate in a Certificate of Citizenship.

But standard procedure for people like us was different. We were supposed to travel to Honolulu. The U.S. Passport Agency there was specifically set up at that time to handle the passport and Certificate of Citizenship application requirements of expatriate families. But I couldn't believe the route I would have to take to get there. I would have to fly to Beijing, then to L.A., then halfway *back* across the Pacific only to have to turn around a few days later and repeat the three-legged race. Six long flights in the space of a week with a baby who hardly knew she was my baby and did not sleep like a baby was not my idea of a good idea.

Because kids change flying.

. . . .

I remembered what the old days were like. Leisure and bliss, that's what. Stroll down aisle. Find seat. Arrange optimal carry-on access. Sit. Close eyes. Nap? Or read. Gaze out the window. Yum, is that airplane food I smell? (My wife says I'm abnormal for looking forward to meals on planes.) Nap or read some more. Listen to music. While eating. Or reading. Go crazy and do all three. Land. Stretch, grab carry-on, deplane, arrive. Refreshed.

That was life before Enoch. After he'd come along, our first flight had been home for Christmas when he was five months old. In those days, just getting out of the house with him was a challenge. Doing it with luggage and then having to check it all in at the airport? It hardly felt familiar to anything I'd done before. We had way too much stuff. I started getting flustered as we stumble-bumble-fumbled through security. Up went the stress a few more notches when I looked at the time and saw we would have to hurry if we were going to make it. I tried to think what day it was, and if it was the same one we'd left home on. As we speed-clunked to our gate with our carry-ons, I felt irritated with every person standing remotely in my way. We arrived to find the flight had already boarded. The airline staff took our stubs and hustled us through.

We arrived at the mouth of the plane aisle, and panic set in. I squinted toward our seats. Had nobody seen all our stuff? Why hadn't we been pre-boarded?

Oh right, late. But how are we supposed to get all this stuff back there? And another thing, what is WRONG *with us? People have been having kids since like forever—it doesn't seem it should be this hard.*

I glanced at little Enoch's face. Oblivious.

Buddy, you cannot walk, you cannot talk, and bringing you has turned

83

this into a trip like no other I've ever taken.

Babies, who really cannot do anything that might be called… useful, have luggage and accessory requirements rivaling those of a touring Maharaja. I was baptized that day. In spite of having been warned ahead of time by more people than I could count, I came to know deep in my soul right there on that plane: my life really was never going to be the same. Sure, the change kids make would later become an expected, welcome part of life, a humorous familiarity, a point of commonality with friends and strangers alike. But that day was revelation itself as The Question was born. I came to call it The Mantra Question. No father forgets his first encounter with The Mantra Question:

> *How can one…little person…require*
> *all*
> *this*
> *stuff?*

We pushed, pulled, lifted, and wrestled Mr. Maharaja's stuff down the aisle. A stroller (you could bring them in those days!), Tammy's carry-on, Tammy's purse, the diaper bag, a toy bag, loose toys, Enoch's blankie, Enoch's carry-on, a sippy cup, my carry-on. I vowed the next time to get serious. Either go all the way and bring that kitchen sink, or else eliminate my own stuff entirely. If I couldn't wear it, I would leave it. Or burn it.

We inched closer to our seats, banging a cadence to my chanting while I willed four consecutive empty overhead bins into being. When at last we got to our row, I checked our seat mates for cobwebs and began formulating a plan for hoisting the stockpile overhead. Then it hit me: the baby.

What am I supposed to do with the baby?

I had no plan, I had no experience. The floor?

No, I don't think I can put him on the floor.

The flight attendants were seating other stragglers. Tammy and I needed all four hands in our scramble to get stowed before takeoff. What was that wonderful smell coming from the galley?

Forget that! Focus.

I scanned wildly for a friendly face. A guy three rows back made eye contact. Good enough. I got to him in one leap.

"WouldyoumindholdinghimforaminutewhileIputawayall-hisstuffhaha?"

In later years, in optimistic moods, I would most of the time be almost definitely fairly sure that I had waited for his response before leaving Enoch in his arms.

I was back to Tammy in a flash and we got everything overhead in record time, triumphantly utilizing a final scrap of luggage to wedge tight the travel stroller that had been refusing to stay up. Then I saw her face: vexed. Extremely vexed. Not at falling strollers, but at failing husbands, husbands who passed off offspring to strangers. So I found a bin door latch that didn't need tinkering and tinkered, which blocked mom's access to the aisle; she sat. I leapt. I found our son gazing into the wide grin of his benefactor, his chubby super-white hands contentedly patting big black cheeks.

"Thanks, man," I said.

His laugh and loud "No problem" drew chuckles from everyone around.

I plopped my sweating self into a seat at last, and now had thoughts only for my defense. I needed something…witty. To create a diversion, to save my skin in the coming onslaught. But a sideways glance revealed the danger had passed. In spite of her best efforts, the corners of Tammy's mouth were turning up and she shook her head. The laughter had already saved me.

. . . .

I determined to come up with a better plan than Hawaii for getting that passport.

Failing to locate any documentation advising me I could avoid Honolulu, I analyzed the law myself, and it seemed to permit walking into any regional passport agency for a passport, even without a Certificate of Citizenship. If I went to Seattle, I'd save us two transfers and two flights and have transoceanic legs that were shorter by two hours. I pulled the trigger on round trip tickets.

I allotted myself four days. Step one would be customs at the Seattle airport. Assuming successful submission of the adoption packet there, step two would be the passport. Step three would be an overnight envelope to the Chinese Embassy in Washington, DC for a tourist visa. That's it. The embassy had same-day service, so I even had one day of cushion.

My plan was fabulous.

The closer the trip got, the more nervous I became.

My plan was harebrained.

The greatest worry wasn't the overly optimistic itinerary. It was that adoption packet. The success of my entire trip hinged upon the U.S. Customs officer to whom I would hand that packet. We'd been given it—already sealed—while in Guangzhou, but the customs officer could still reject it. What if he required the documents for non-residents that we hadn't done? Hours of research and emailing boiled down to one irrefutable reality: I had no guarantee of success. My eroding confidence held on for dear life to the Child Citizenship Act of 2000. My personal interpretation of that law was that we qualified for automatic citizenship status upon landing in the U.S. I just didn't know if the customs officer would see it the same way.

Passing through customs was not the only land mine. My visit to the Seattle Regional Passport Agency had its own potential dead ends. According to the laws in effect at that time, two government agencies had the power to grant citizenship to our daughter. United States Citizenship and Immigration Services (USCIS) could grant it with a Certificate of Citizenship, and the Department of State could grant it with a passport. Standard operating procedure was doing the Certificate of Citizenship before the passport, and doing the reverse was not the norm according to anything I could find. The law permitted it, but I didn't know if this passport agency would do it.

I needed an expert. We had met the Vice Consul of the U.S. Consulate in Guangzhou during our adoption ceremony, and now she became the most helpful, communicative, and accessible government official I had ever had the pleasure to encounter. She answered all my questions via email, then asked me a list of her own. She walked me through figuring out exactly how our complicated residence realities might be interpreted by the law. In the end, she could only tell me that it was possible for my trip to succeed, but even she could make no guarantees. Everything depended on naturalization at the border, and that depended on the acceptance of the packet. I was comforted that, even though the border officer technically held the authority to reject it, the Vice Consul had never heard of an adopted child being turned back at the border.

My ace in the hole was an official letter she provided me. In that letter she asserted that, based upon the authority of her office as well as her consultation with USCIS Guangzhou, the irregularities of our residence situation did not preclude us from receiving the same interpretation under the law as those with more traditional forms of permanent resident status. I placed the letter in its own plastic sleeve and strapped it to the packet.

The day of the trip arrived. Bad news came hours before leaving. My travel document service in Washington, DC informed me that the Chinese Embassy had suspended same-day processing until further notice. Unless they reinstated it, I would have to settle for next-day service. There went my one day of cushion. A second email arrived after we were airborne, which I read after deplaning in Seattle. It was from the Vice Consul, and this one—phew—was good news:

> I heard from the Seattle Passport Agency Customer Service Manager again this morning. He told me he would inform the counter staff that you were coming and of your situation (no Certificate of Citizenship). Now you can focus on getting the visa. Please let me know how it's working out.
>
> Hope the two of you had a nice flight.

Amazingly, we had. I had gotten on our domestic flight discouraged to see it full, only to have the one empty seat turn up next to me. I was grateful for the use of two seats even though we'd bought only one. On the international leg we were even more blessed, and had a bulkhead with a bassinet. I couldn't believe my good fortune when the ten-hour flight turned out to be lots of sleeping and little crying.

Our plane had taxied to the Sea-Tac Airport gate in a light rain (go figure), and I'd experienced the oddity of extreme nervousness about crossing my own country's border. But we sailed through customs with no issues whatsoever, and nothing was asked but the most basic of questions. The Certificate of Citizenship would not be scheduled to arrive at our permanent U.S. address for weeks, but the process was underway.

My anxiety switched over to my morning passport appointment. I could imagine a dozen nightmarish scenarios. From baggage claim I called the travel document service in DC. The moratorium on same-day service had not been lifted as I'd hoped, but they were confident next-day service would still get us the visa in time.

My in-laws picked us up. They were so excited about their new little granddaughter that they'd traveled across the country to see her. Their assistance over the next few days would be invaluable as I tried to coordinate a baby schedule with all my running around. Eden and I wouldn't be making the switch to local time. I refused to add jet lag in a one-year old to my burdens, or to those of my wife the following week, so the plan was to stay on China time and sleep all day. Except for me. Since I had to take care of business during business hours, I would fit in sleep where I could.

As soon as we arrived at our hosts' home, I told them I had an overnight envelope to be mailed. It was addressed to the USCIS Indianapolis Field Office; I had to change our address of record. Their system still listed our Indiana address where we'd compiled the dossier while matched with Lily. My hosts were headed out anyway, so they offered to drop the mailer in an overnight box for me. With that taken care of, we travelers headed off to bed for an abbreviated sleep, with an alarm set to get us up before our hosts went to bed.

Early the next morning local time, having whiled away a long, quiet night in a house with nothing to speak of for entertaining a one-year-old, I was downtown at the passport agency. I had an 8AM appointment, the first of the day and procured online at the earliest allowable date weeks earlier. I left my pockets' contents with the guards, passed through the metal detectors, went upstairs to the second floor waiting area, and sat down to await several other customers bewilderingly ahead of me. When my number was called, I went to the counter and stated my name. A blank look. I gave it again, smoothly dropping the Vice Consul's as well. Same look.

Ah yes, I'm in the right place, welcome home. I hadn't enjoyed home-grown government service in quite some time.

"Ask your supervisor," I barked through a smile.

He did call over the supervisor, and her response all but laid me out on the floor: "Yes, could you repeat your name, please? We have nothing on record. The Consulate in which country, did you say?"

Oh, my.

I was going to have to explain everything from the absolute beginning. Where was this "Manager" of so-called Customer Service, anyway? Had he dared lie to my precious Vice Consul? They truly knew nothing, whether I could believe it or not, of my coming. Now I didn't even have the confidence this supervisor would hear me out, so I started talking, and quick. I began somewhere in the middle and verbalized a timeline evolving in either direction with details as they came to me. Coherence, even chronology, would have served me better, but then another thought would turn to words before I could stop myself. I longed to start over.

Is she even listening?

Her eyes were locked on my whirring lips, but through the glass partition I couldn't decide if they were intent or vacuous.

Is she evaluating me? Psychiatrically?

Finally I warmed her to a point where I could tell she'd upgraded me to non-frightening. Then she started asking questions. We discussed the Child Citizenship Act of 2000. I took out the Vice Consul's letter. There was nothing in the law, I dared assert right to her face, preventing her from issuing our daughter a U.S. Passport without a Certificate of Citizenship in hand. Perhaps true, she said, but neither had she ever known anyone to try asking. She seemed reticent, reluctant, perhaps, to act on interpretations of the law from some guy walking in off the street. No matter how non-frightening he might be.

"Where's your daughter?"

Uh-oh, another irregularity. Here I was applying for a passport and I hadn't even brought the applicant.

"She's sleeping. We were in China yesterday." I looked at my watch. "It's one in the morning to us."

The thought of our entire trip being reduced to futility at the place where I was supposed to have had the red carpet rolled out for me made me ill. We couldn't even return to China if I failed to get a passport. The Vice Consul had warned me in no uncertain terms not to return to China on the Chinese passport, its dearly-bought U.S. visa canceled. I'd been so eager to avoid Honolulu, I'd made nothing even resembling a backup plan.

The Vice Consul was my savior. One last time the supervisor looked over her letter, then made her decision. She would approve my application. The passport would be issued. I practically kissed the Vice Consul's letter before lovingly placing it back in its sleeve. I would never know whether or not my own arguments could have prevailed without it.

"But it is mandatory, Mr. Johnson, that I see your daughter before I release the passport. Be here with her this afternoon at 2:00."

Understood. I breathed relief.

Passport, check.

That afternoon I could overnight it to Washington, the visa could be applied for the following day, it would be issued on the day after that, and then overnighted back to me. The next morning we'd catch our flight to Beijing. My plan was looking as stupendous as I always knew it had been.

That afternoon at 2:00 I sat back down at the same window. I'd already picked out a FedEx store we could walk to and not have to bother with the car. I carried an addressed overnight envelope in my hand. It required only the beautiful, stiff United States passport of the cutie sitting in my lap.

"Hi, yes, passport pickup please? Eden Johnson."

"Oh, we didn't issue any passports today. Our systems are down."

"Excuse me, what? I have to have this passport to get a visa so we can go back to China. The rest of our family is there. We fly on Friday."

"I'm so sorry, sir. The passport processing systems of the United States Department of State are down around the world. No one anywhere got a passport today."

"You are kidding! When will the systems be up? Does this happen often?"

The supervisor saw me and came over. She spoke kindly. "I am so, so sorry. I wish there were something I could do." She knew how badly I needed that passport, but she was powerless. Since there'd never been a system-wide failure in her tenure, she couldn't say how long it would last. She assured me that government people were working on it.

How comforting.

I could tell from her face and body language she'd been dealing with irate customers already, so I said no more and wished her well in her crisis. She assured me our application would be at the front of the queue[22] and promised to call the moment there was news. As I wrote down my hosts' number for her then turned to leave, she proffered a terrifying, "I hope tomorrow?"

My grand plan had just been smacked back to foolhardy. Worse, its last, gasping hope was the computer savvy of the federal government. I tottered back to the car in disbelief, desperate for a nap. It was almost time to get up.

I thought I'd just lain down and it *was* time to get up. We were up in time for supper. I forced meat and potatoes into a body craving eggs and toast or cereal. When my hosts went to bed, I strapped a borrowed car seat into the car they had made available to us for the week, and drove the night streets of northern Seattle. We stumbled on a Walgreens in Ballard and went inside to kill time. For hours we walked those aisles, and it wouldn't be our only time that week. Colorful American trinkets and candy made good gifts for my kids back home and decent entertainment for the one in the cart. But it was Walgreens, not Disney, so I was relieved when the minute hand had completed enough rotations to justify creeping toward home. Somewhere before dawn I was allowed to finally listen to my body yelling at me to go to bed. A second moonlit day successfully whiled away.

I hadn't been asleep anything close to eight hours when the phone rang with the call that systems were up. The supervisor had gotten her first-person visual the day before, so I could pick up the passport alone. My father-in-law rushed me downtown one last time and parked the car while I ran inside. At last I held the gorgeous, crisp, navy booklet.

Passport, check. For real.

My plan still had a chance. Same-day visas had not been reinstated, but my one remaining ray of hope was to get the passport back the same morning we flew. If it arrived early enough, we might be able to make our 11:00 AM flight. I marked "first delivery" on the FedEx waybill and paid the high fee. Delivery was promised by 8:00 AM. Sealing the envelope, I dropped our lives in the outgoing mail. All I could do now was pray.

The next two days, which otherwise could have been filled with rest, were filled attempting to reach USCIS. First with Indianapolis then with Buffalo, I frantically sought confirmation that our change of address had gone through. I knew our old Indiana house was standing empty, and I could not risk our nearly irreplaceable Certificate of Citizenship being sent there.

By the final afternoon I had done nothing but listen to recorded menus and leave messages. I knew before they began that every menu would be useless to me, but I had no choice but to listen through to their termini in hopes of one time being given the option to speak with a real person. I never was, regardless of how many points at which I tried pressing "0."

I quit and went to bed, only to have my host wake me a few hours later. USCIS Buffalo was on the phone, a connection miracle on the magnitude of Horton hearing a Who.[23] And the news was good: they'd received the change of address form. Double bonus, our immigration packet had arrived from U.S. Customs as well. The man I spoke with was helpful, gracious, and friendly—service purportedly available to all potential citizens requiring personalized attention from USCIS in a justified and unusual case. The catch must be surviving their menu recordings. I hung up and would have shouted for joy if I hadn't been right next to the crib. The Certificate of Citizenship was still on track.

Our final night held time for one last romp through Walgreens and then home for an early sleep. I was up with the sun, waiting for 8:00 and the delivery of the passport with its freshly-minted China visa. But 8:00 came and no delivery truck. 8:02. 8:05. 8:09. 8:14. It was a full hyperventilating half-hour before it showed. The ink was still drying on my signature for the courier as our car peeled out of the neighborhood. But we made it. I checked my bag, bought the one-way infant ticket I had not been able to purchase any earlier because the name on the ticket had not yet legally existed, and found our gate. Sitting back in my seat during takeoff, I did not congratulate myself. My plan had bordered on idiocy; it was ludicrous that I'd expected it to work. Had it really only been four days? It felt like ten. I turned to our family's newest American citizen and said, "Eden, it's nothing short of a miracle we're sitting here on this flight.

"Now Daddy needs some sleep."

All Roads Lead to Beijing

生而知之者，上也
学而知之者，次也
困而学之，又其次也
困而不学，民斯为下矣

By three methods we may learn wisdom:
First, by reflection, which is noblest;
Second, by imitation, which is easiest;
And third, by experience, which is the bitterest.

Confucius

IT HAD BEEN ONE thing to inquire after Lily when our official connection to her was recent. It was another to keep beating at doors half-a-year later. However, because I already had to write to Ivy about my Seattle trip (it would trigger all of our post-placement paperwork), I decided to slip in a mention of our continued curiosity about Liu Hai Rou. Was she still in Beijing or had she been sent back to her orphanage to be matched? Had she been matched already? When she was matched, would it be with a family from our same agency? I told Ivy we wanted the future family of Liu Hai Rou to have access to our story if that's what they wanted. After all, it would be their daughter's history.

Ivy said Liu Hai Rou was still in the foster home and still improving. She was eating table food, walking fast, starting to speak. Her orphanage had recently submitted the updated paperwork that would make her re-eligible for adoption. Ivy couldn't say whether the new file would end up with them or not. It could be given to any agency. She offered to keep us updated if that's what we would like. Absolutely we would like that, I wrote back after we'd devoured and reread every word three times.

Lily would have a family soon. A family was what she needed, right?

We guessed she might leave Beijing before summer.

We had summer Beijing plans ourselves, though nothing to do with Lily; we were going to the Great Wall. Tammy's niece, Carrie, had been interning at our culture center that semester, and we told her she had to give the Wall a second chance. Six years earlier as a pre-teen, she'd visited it with us and her grandparents. That day had been miserable. We rode the cable car in a freezing gale that, once we were outside, all but removed clothing from the body. We lasted five minutes. Carrie needed a better Wall memory.

So did our kids.

Their visit had been longer ago during a May holiday. We'd barely seen the Wall at all, as the people teeming on it looked like ants on a…well, whatever it is they're on, you can only see the ants. As we were carried along from point A to point B, the throng around us was only slightly more delighted with their national treasure than they were with Enoch's blond hair and white cheeks. He was like an alternate tourist attraction, only free. "Hey, let's all feel the blinding-white foreign child here in this backpack carrier. Here, take my picture with it!" Unfathomably, his fright only added to their entertainment.

As far as Enoch was concerned, if we were talking about *that* wall again, it was the furthest thing from great.

But a summer trip without crowds was better in every way for everyone. Enoch and Haddie had all the space they wanted for playing pirate, princess, fort, and ninja. Elijah wore himself out toddling and climbing on the endless "rocks." Eden, as always, preferred the nearness of the backpack sling. We'd had a hard time believing it at first, but she would draw as much attention as the other kids had in their day. We got to eavesdrop on many a debate over how we'd produced such different looking kids. Others would discern the real story, which only multiplied the attention. Or the ludicrous opinion would be shouted down, "You think the girl is Chinese? Look how she's dressed, look how she plays! Ha!"

Following our excursion to the Wall, we took a day to play in a city park that had a wave pool. I sat with Tammy in the grass while the kids splashed and played in a sandy beach area. It had been one year since we'd moved back to China. A full year since our summer of loss. I looked out over the skyline surrounding the park and imagined one of those buildings housing Lily's foster home. It fascinated me to scrutinize them, though the odds of her home being right there in sight had to be nil. I got to wondering where in the huge city it actually was.

"You know, dear," I commented aloud, "she moved here to this city almost exactly a year ago now."

We looked at each other and unexpectedly got emotional. Imagining Lily close by got to us like had not happened in some time. But maybe she wasn't close. Maybe she'd already gone back. Maybe she'd already been matched. Maybe she was adopted already.

On impulse I decided to call. Ivy was just across town. I had her cell number.

She picked up and I started explaining who I was, as we'd only spoken the one time I'd been to the office six months prior. But she knew me right away. And yes, since our inquiry two months earlier, Liu Hai Rou had gotten completely well and gone back to her orphanage. She might be matched at any time. I hung up and remained sitting in the grass, watching my kids play.

I no longer scanned the skyline.

There was no one there I cared about.

. . . .

As quickly as it'd come, emotion over Lily receded. Looking back over the whole saga, I could admit it was always going to end as it had. The memory of Lily was taking its place as a piece of the past. A year is a long time. We had grown to be grateful that Lily had recovered so fully. Back home in Xi'an again, attaching to Eden had us fully engaged. And though she certainly dispensed daily confirmation that we'd been unprepared for the difficulties of adoptive parenting, never did we feel like we would've rather had Lily instead. Our daughter was Eden. We loved her. And slowly we found the literature to help us understand that our struggles were common.

Lily was a beloved memory, a painful memory, a girl we had loved and lost. We hoped her forever family would come soon, and we fully accepted that it wasn't us. I recoiled at the thought of calling the agency any more. In fact, I determined I wouldn't call again until I was calling for the last time. I would wait long enough to be sure her adoption was final.

She quit coming up.

Eden celebrated her second birthday (her first with us) and our one year anniversary of meeting her in the referral email. We closed the coffee shop for the afternoon and invited everyone we knew to a costume party. Our family went as the Fellowship of the Ring. We dressed Eden as The Precious[24], all black clothes with a thick gold band around her middle, complete with Black Speech inscription, "One ring to rule them all."

We laughed at its accuracy, seeing as how the girl wearing it had been ruling us for the past eleven months.

. . . .

I had to go to Beijing, again.

An entire year after we'd finalized, and still the paperwork was pummeling me in the face. But this trip was because of stupidity.

My own.

The entire journey had been necessitated only because of one little mis-tick of one little checkbox on one little form. Out of scores of forms and hundreds of questions, I'd mis-marked one box. Now I had to fly two-and-a-half hours to Beijing to fix it.

The question had been simple: did I desire, and authorize, the U.S. Department of State to forward my child's information on to the Social Security Administration? Check the "Yes" box, and the SSA would receive her information and assign her a Social Security number automatically. Check the "No" box, and...well, who would do that?

Morons, that's who. That easy of a question, and I'd flunked.

Without a Social Security number, for tax purposes our family still numbered five. Without a Social Security number, there would be no adoption credit. Without a Social Security number, do not pass Go and do not collect $200. No, I would spend it instead, and more, traveling to Beijing. I could have spent two seconds and two drops of ink, but ended up spending two weeks kicking myself. And boy, there is nothing quite like self-flagellation to make a long trip loom larger.

But when the day came, and I had a few books on a Kindle,

some of that old love for solo travel came back: I was able to spend the flight, the taxi ride, lunch, my walk to the embassy, and the time in line…reading.

All applications for Social Security numbers made by U.S. citizens living in China are submitted in person (exception: people who know how to tick checkboxes) to the U.S. Embassy in Beijing. The embassy then forwards those applications to the U.S. Social Security Administration in Manila for processing. I was nervous, not wanting to commit any further gaffes, but the lady who took my application said everything looked good. Unfortunately, it would be six months, clear into another tax year, before I could expect to hear anything back from the Philippines.

But at least with good reading in hand the day hadn't been a total waste. I headed to the airport on the new airport train, hoping to beat the heavy traffic on the highway. I did. I arrived early.

Super, more reading time.

When the train doors opened and no one moved, I briefly thought it odd, but my book was just at a good part. I figured we were waiting on another train or something. The doors shut after another five minutes of reading, and then to my panic the train started moving backwards.

We are LEAVING?

Sure enough, we emerged outside again, and into view came the gargantuan orange roof of Terminal Three.[25]

What on earth? Surely I could not have been so engrossed in my book as to have thought no one got off when really they did, and these are all new people?

But all the luggage was the same. The people had to be the same.

Surely this many people would not come to the airport without wanting to also stay at the airport? Think, Dann, think.

My mind scrambled to construct any believable scenario that could make sense of people training to an airport and not getting off. I couldn't.

Why not ask someone?

Glancing around, it was easy to see no one looked remotely as lost as I felt. Clearly my best bet was to figure things out for myself. What a relief to have no wife along to cast aspersions on this fine plan. But I had no time to dwell on what she might have said. With a receding T3 as my reference point, and while craning my neck in all directions as I concentrated on looking nonchalant, I figured it out. We weren't leaving, we were carving a huge arc toward Terminal Two.[26] How unfortunate to have no wife along as witness to my triumph.

I would have to get off at T2 and figure out how to work my way back to T3. I (finally) bowed to the wiser conventions of my wife and asked for directions. I employed my ability to speak the language and learned of a shuttle bus, which I readily boarded. (Mention of a laborious side-trip through and stop at Terminal One was conspicuously missing from my informant's counsel.) When the shuttle finally pulled up to the doors of T3, I was kicking myself anew for having to employ another ability of mine, namely that of running pell-mell, to make my flight at all. Barely.

I flew home believing that at least my adoption troubles had finally reached their end.

. . . .

The culture center got busier. I became the general manager. Our employees went from countable on two fingers to more than were countable on two hands. Life happened, kids grew. The days on which I thought of Lily grew further apart. When people asked if we wanted more kids, if I would consider adopting again, I always answered the same way. "Nope, we're done. Four is enough, and once is enough." But then one time, on a retreat with our culture center staff, hiking along a mountain river looking for a bonfire spot, something different came out. A co-worker walking behind me asked that same question, and I heard my, "No, we're done" followed five steps later by an, "Unless it's Lily."

I didn't know why I'd said it. She would be adopted soon, if she wasn't already. We no longer knew anything, truly. But a few days later I repeated the sentiment in a journal entry. It's one of three—and only three—times I mentioned Lily in my journal during the second year after we lost her.

> So tired today. I know these years while the kids are young will be the most tiring. Or at least I hope that's the case. We are getting too old to keep up this pace—I do not think we will grow this family any more. Unless, of course, there would open a door that led to Lily Anne. She is closer to 3 than 2 now. Where is she? How is she?

> I was just playing with Eden a few minutes ago before putting her to bed. We whispered together in the dark, and I told her how far she's come. It is absolutely amazing to look back on. The end of this month we'll have had her for one year.

The other two entries, a few weeks apart, came several months later:

> Tax day. Lily Day. The day we got the phone call. Where is she, Lord? We are happy to know she healed well, but we would love to know what happened to her and where she is now.

> I noticed on my to-do list the form from the grant office. It reminded me of our continued hope and search for Lily. God, do a miracle. Allow us to find out what happened to our Lily.

So early on in our process that we'd gotten it while still in the States, we'd gotten an adoption grant of a few thousand dollars when still matched with Lily. My to-do list task was writing up some thoughts and submitting pictures to the organization who had given it.[27] Though everything was of Eden, it had triggered thoughts of Lily.

Our "search" for Lily consisted pretty much of web searches for her Chinese name, along with flimsy hopes her new family might contact us out of the blue. Every time we looked, we hoped something would turn up, but nothing ever did.

I think reluctance to ask our former agency about her had become subconscious fear it would only confirm they had no information, either.

Relentless Father

TAMMY DOESN'T SPEAK OF Lily in the second year after our loss any more than I do. Life's routines carry us forward as they always have. One of Tammy's routines is a monthly get-together with other foreign women connected to the culture center. The group is currently working their way through an audio study together, meeting in one of the culture center's unused classrooms.

Tammy listens to the night's lesson while staring idly at the group's knitter and wondering why someone didn't buy the DVD version instead. Suddenly the teacher asks a question which so arrests Tammy's attention that for the rest of the night she has no further issues with concentration. She leaves for home as soon as things wrap up. It has started raining, and she picks her way back to our complex through puddles. After hanging her wet stuff on our hall tree, she gets a cup of hot water[28] and sits down on the couch to share with me about her evening. I'm doing some work on the computer just before bed, half-listening.

"So at my study tonight, dear, the teacher challenged us to believe God for something. You know, something big. Ask him to move a mountain. Ask for something really out there, something I would normally say was totally impossible."

Like Enoch turning in neat homework?

Eden falling asleep at night?

I know. Shorter work meetings.

Half thoughts come out the side of my mouth.

"Honey, this is serious, listen. As soon as the teacher said what she said, I felt in my heart that God was asking me to believe him for something specific. I want to ask what you think he might have said. Guess what I felt led to ask him for. To believe him for."

I make eye contact. I have not thought of her in some time. But I know.

"That he'd give us Lily."

What I do not know is that Tammy has questioned herself all the way home, eventually designating me as a sort of fleece to check against what she thinks she's heard. We are going through two or three obvious difficulties at the time, any of which I might have offered as my guess. Instead I have bowled her over, not only by answering as I have, but as quickly as I have, without pause.

We look at each other for half a minute. Neither says anything further.

Peculiar, that wall clock. So loud.

Odd feelings are kindled in me. I cannot identify, nor shake them.

. . . .

The girl we first called "daughter" in China was neither Eden nor Lily.

Our first jobs in China, back when we'd had only two kids, were in Chongqing, a city which I described to everyone back home as "the biggest city you've never heard of," though it would become more well-known in subsequent years. When we moved there, it had recently become China's inaugural inland municipality, directly under Beijing and no longer part of Sichuan Province. The transformations being rendered by road-building alone were mind-numbing, and money poured in for infrastructure projects as far as the eye could see. To me, the city was already reminiscent of Manhattan—skyscrapers thronging along rivers, endless bigness—but Chongqing had only begun to grow.

Tammy and I had been hired by a consulting firm that ran trainings across a wide range of professional and scientific fields but also coordinated some orphan care for a Hong Kong nonprofit. The latter interested us. We worked with educational bureaus in the remote county areas of Chongqing where no orphanages existed, directly sponsoring individual children. Almost none had been orphaned in infancy, but rather lost their parents in a road accident or other tragedy later on in childhood. In general, they lived with someone connected to their family, a relative or a friend, though some had become the primary family caretakers of aged grandparents themselves. Every year we conducted retreats for about fifty kids, and they ranged from age five to perhaps eleven, though as the years passed the older kids stayed on.

The retreats were a short time of escape and fun, a camp experience where we filled them up with as much love as possible in a few days. We educated them in self-care, in nutrition, in staying safe, and about other things children learn from their parents. On some retreats we brought doctors or a dentist and provided checkups, teeth cleanings, and health and hygiene education. Every retreat, we had the same group. Every retreat ended with tears. On both sides.

Tammy and I grew especially close to Yao Shu Ting, a ten-year-old girl that over time we came to call our *"gan* daughter," something like an informal goddaughter. Yao Shu Ting was not a girl we could have ever adopted, not that we ever discussed it seriously. None of the orphans we worked with were adoptable, certainly not internationally. None had the paperwork, nor were they ever likely to.

Yao Shu Ting lived near the town where we did the retreats, and she lived alone. These more than anything were the reasons we grew closest to her. Everyone else bussed in to the retreats from hours around, and we never saw them otherwise. She lived right off the highway into town, and we stopped to see her any time we drove through. She lived in a small cinder block house with one main room and a kitchen. She prepared her own meals. She had moved in at age nine. I once brought my parents, visiting from the States, to her home as we passed by on a family vacation together, an experience that touched them deeply and which they still talk about. But it was doubtlessly forgettable for Yao Shu Ting. Her convenient location meant she got many visitors.

One visiting group we brought in paid for a ceiling to be hung in her little house, presumably for warmth.[29] I wondered how much hotter the summers were going to get, because no one else in the village had chipboard ceilings installed. But I didn't know if that was because they couldn't afford them or just preferred the airflow. Westerners who have spent any time with Chinese know of their love for open windows, regardless of season. Freezing to death would be nothing to the villainy of stale air.

We'd been visiting Yao Shu Ting for almost two years before an aunt in town, who I'd also only just learned about, dropped a bombshell on us when she mentioned that the parents weren't dead, you know. No, I did not know. Horrified, we strove to imagine what could lead parents to abandon their own nine-year-old to live on her own. We later learned it was a baby brother. They could only keep one of them.

We were never going to be like parents to Yao Shu Ting. It didn't matter how much compassion and fondness we had for her, two or three visits a year did not make us significant people in her life. Part of us wished we could bring her to live with us. But not really, as that would have been quite difficult on her. What she really needed was a local family to take her in as one of their own. Still, we wished our connections could have been more frequent, and more significant. But in the end we were only two more in a long line of the well-intentioned but ultimately non-providers of all she truly needed, destined to recede into the background.

One time we did have the privilege of hosting Yao Shu Ting for a few days in our home in the big city. She was there for an appointment with an eye specialist. Tammy was giddy to have her, especially as the visit fortuitously coincided with Shu Ting's 12th birthday. We took full advantage and made it memorable. At least for one birthday in her lonely pre-teen life she would be surrounded by a family who loved her.

We went to the zoo. Our seven- and five-year-olds had made more zoo visits than they could remember, but for Yao Shu Ting and baby Elijah it was a first. We toured every corner of the place as a family of six, then topped off the day with a momentous dinner of Kentucky Fried Chicken and cake. The shy birthday girl seemed perpetually embarrassed, but never could wipe the smile from her face, either.

Our second day with her was even better. The awkward newness was replaced with simple play time with our kids, a walk in the city, and going to a mall. The top floor had an ice rink, and after a shaky, laugh-filled start—Yao Shu Ting's first experience with skating—she took to it fabulously. She posed for many pictures over the next two hours, and when our time was up, we had a hard time getting her off the ice.

Her visit was over almost before it started, but she was missing her regular life. Our loud house had to feel foreign and uncomfortable compared to her normal solitude. It was time to take her home. I would accompany her on the ten-hour bus trip the next day.

I have fond, almost fatherly memories of Yao Shu Ting from that trip. Without Tammy and the kids around she did even less talking than usual. I tried chatting for a little while, but it was easy to see we both preferred the silence of looking out the windows. At lunch, we ate our instant noodles squatting side by side in the dirt next to the bus. I am squat-challenged. Maintaining that position for a whole meal worked up an appetite almost faster than the incoming noodles could compensate for.

The farther we got from the city the poorer the roads got. And more mountainous. On one of the stops to add water for the brakes, I went inside the roadside store to find spicy peanuts or spicy dried tofu. Packaged pickled chicken feet caught my eye, and on a hunch I bought one for Yao Shu Ting. Had I had known how fast she'd gnaw it clean, I'd have bought her half a dozen. I sampled a bite when she offered it, but I've never been able to nibble those things without having uncomfortable visions of their previous life tramping a chicken yard. I was happier just enjoying my *gan* daughter's lip-smacking. I got pensive as I watched her, and thought about her life, trying to imagine what it must be like. I couldn't. The dissimilarities between her and me at age twelve were too great. It was those gaps, more than her shyness, more than my standard, unnatural Mandarin and her Sichuan dialect, that hindered conversation. We were from different worlds.

She finished the foot and I offered my headphones for a listen. The flavor of the moment happened to be Bryan White, the Dixie Chicks, Colin Raye. In my youth, such a genre would not have been found in[30] any music device in my vicinity. In fact, in 1980's suburban Chicago I can recall hearing no answer to the question, "What kind of music do you like?" more often than I heard, "All kinds. Except country."

Funnily enough, the first place I moved after marrying a girl from Pennsylvania was Texas. I had grown up traveling extensively every summer because my dad was a high school math teacher,[31] but I'd never traveled south. I didn't even have a frame of reference for a place like Texas. On our move down, we hadn't even exited the southern end of the state in which I'd spent my entire life before Tammy and I started hearing a dialect of English I'd only ever heard on television. Once we hit Texas the culture shock was complete. I wouldn't be that traumatized when we went to teach English in Taiwan three years later.

Texas seemed unaware that there were kinds of music other than country. Country music played in the mall, it psyched the stadium, it headlined the fair, it blared from every car. Or would have, had there been any cars. We had a car, but everything else on the road was a pickup truck. And, as we were the Yankee morons who had brought down a car without a working air conditioner, our windows were always open and we could hear everyone else's music that much better. We had cassette tapes of non-country music, but they caused more rubbernecking than our rolled-down windows, or melted in the heat. We left them home.

Amazingly, we adjusted. Culture shock wore off, my stereo-types faded, and Texas became home. And I'm fixin' to tell y'all, it changed us more than we changed it, that's for dang sure. That day on the bus with Yao Shu Ting, the country music I offered her had been put there by me. But now it was her turn to react for all the world like she was from 1980's suburban Chicago. She took those headphones off in less than five seconds.

"No, wait, Shu Ting, try this next track. How about that?"

Her face politely grimaced a thanks but no thanks.

Maybe it was just foreign music in general she didn't like. I switched genres. There went that theory. Her eyes lit up at a little-known group playing self-titled "astro rock." She waved her hand furiously at me to stop, and that was the last I heard from her. She listened contentedly through both their albums until we arrived.

I may have lived seven years in Texas and have twang-apprecia-tive kids of my own, but one unchanging truth had just been laid down: I would forever have at least one daughter who would never be a fan of country music. We got off the bus and I walked my *gan* daughter across the parking lot to her aunt. I passed her off with smiles and waves. And more than a little unease about what the future held for her.

I never saw her again.

We've never stopped trying to find her.

. . . .

Our ties to Lily had been exponentially beyond compassion and fondness. She had been our real daughter. I couldn't understand the father love God had put in my heart for Lily, nor why it seemed to keep hanging around. She was gone. She was going to belong to someone else. Quite possibly already did. We wanted to find out where, and didn't know if we ever would. Memories of Yao Shu Ting haunted us, warning us that Lily, too, might vanish without a trace.

. . . .

Spring turned to summer.

I was swamped at the culture center as we expanded our painfully small kitchen. We cut a doorway in a wall, built out a room, disguised it on the outside as a fireplace, then divided the height of the interior space into two stories of seven feet high each. By also moving the coffee counter out a few feet, we more than tripled our kitchen space.

Our older three started kindergarten, third, and fifth grades. We had not contacted the agency in the year since they'd told us Lily had gone back to her orphanage. The timing had never seemed right, though more than enough time had passed for a completed adoption. The more time went by without hearing anything about her, the more likely it became that we'd lose track of her completely.

Clingy Eden was still having enough post-adoption difficulty to keep our lives full. I stayed home one weekday each week so Tammy could get out and look for her sanity, which was apparently, going by what she brought home each week, hanging out near the shoes or the fabric. Eden did continue to blow us away with her progress, though. Kids from hard places[32] need physiological as well as emotional healing, and though for Eden neither took place overnight, or even in months, they did come. Her days of being a two-year old were numbered. Her princess party with the chocolate cupcakes was around the corner.

We entered our third year of life after Lily.

My pain had faded, and was not a place in my heart I could access easily. Especially that deep, desperate place I'd been the first few days of loss—eyes brimming, emotion quivering just below the surface, ready to break through over nothing—I could no longer remember what that had felt like. It was all gone. That wasn't how I experienced life. Even when I wanted to go back there, and tried to go back there—to feel again what that place had felt like—I couldn't.

It would have been impossible to imagine I was about to live there.

Part III

Hope

Found

God is not deaf, though He be long silent.

Harriet Beecher Stowe

WE WERE THE ONES who found her.

Tammy asked first.

She and Rebecca had been emailing back and forth putting the finishing touches on a post-placement report about Eden.

The pink dress and Eden's chocolate birthday cupcakes had been a week earlier.

Tammy sent the question I had been putting off since the poolside call to Ivy sixteen months earlier: "Is Liu Hai Rou adopted yet?" I didn't know Tammy had asked until I saw Rebecca's reply: She would be glad to check, but could we remind her of the child's social welfare institute and date of birth? I didn't remember the name of Lily's town, either, so I pulled the original referral, over two-and-a-half years old, for the name of the city orphanage. All the old documentation was there. The story sucked me in, and I was caught unawares by my life's greatest loss. It had been a long time. I sat motionless as long-dimmed memories transmuted once again to feeling. I pored over everything before remembering what I'd been looking for. Then I sent Rebecca her information.

We'd waited an inordinately long time; there was no way Liu Hai Rou wasn't adopted by now. Somewhere, Lily was going by a different name in a different family. I just hoped the agency could find her this long after she'd gone back to her orphanage. Her new family might like to hear what we knew about their daughter's history.

Rebecca reported back a few days later that her inquiries about the status of Liu Hai Rou had not gone far. She wasn't listed on the CCCWA website, so they'd asked the CCCWA about her file. The answer came back that it was "frozen." Rebecca didn't even know what that meant. She promised us their staff was investigating. She did hope we'd ultimately be able to learn something, ideally that Liu Hai Rou had long since been matched with a family, but she wasn't exactly optimistic.

"Frozen" didn't make it sound likely.

In the most poignant episode of déjà vu I'd ever known, I thought about Lily all weekend. "Lily" was the first word off my pen when I sat down to journal. I hadn't written her name in eight months.

> Lily has once again been consuming my mind. If she had been adopted, would her file say "frozen"? I wouldn't think so. Is she dying? Lord, are you going to prod me to some action? Am I supposed to take some without prodding? I wonder what would come of me flying to her province, renting a car, and driving out to her city to try and find her?
>
> Is this still grief? Normal? Are you trying to tell us something? If so, I need help.
>
> I've asked for a sign and I'll ask again. When we lost her, if anything became ultimately clear, it's that things had always been hopeless from the start, apart from a miracle from you.
>
> I'd say that hasn't changed.
>
> Tonight I read Isaiah 5. Verse 19 read, "Woe to those who say, 'Let God hurry, let him hasten his work so we may see it.'"
>
> Lord, I realize that we may never find out what's happened to Lily. But I pray that we could. At least know. Even if it means hearing the worst—that she had died—wouldn't that be better than forever not knowing? Maybe it would be worse.
>
> Intervene, God! May it not be the case that she has died! Use us somehow on her behalf before it becomes life and death again! Why save her back then only to have us live to witness her die now?
>
> My human perspective is so limited, I know. Help us just to know what's happened to her, Jesus.

By the next morning I was no less anxious. In a bit of timing that could not have been worse, we got an auto-reply from

Rebecca's computer. She would be out of the office the whole week. No one else there could help us. I dared not contact Beijing, because I didn't know who was in the loop, or even still worked there.

For eight days we feared the worst.

When Rebecca's brief reply came the following week, it was eerily similar to her email just before the first time she'd given us bad news about Lily. It only said she had information, would I please call her that afternoon?

Tears filled my eyes. Lily was dead.

"I have some information for you."

What else could it be that she couldn't write it?

For the second time in as many weeks I was transported to losing her two years earlier. I sat at my desk chair and stared unseeing over the culture center office, the morning's work forgotten. So many times I'd tried to conjure up that old hurt, remember those feelings, almost always failing. Now with one sentence, I no longer had to try.

"I have some information for you."

I already knew what it would be.

I reached Rebecca on her office phone. She surprised me. They'd found Lily. My relief was audible. *She's alive.*

"But why is her file frozen?"

If hearing she was alive had been surprising, what came next stunned me. Lily was in the Beijing foster home that had rescued her as a baby.

Lily's next birthday would be her fourth.

And she is in the exact same place where she was put when taken from us as a baby?

She had never left. She was growing up there.

Why?

I failed to comprehend.

During every memory we have made with Eden, and there are years of them, Lily has been there in that home?

So much time.

Without parents, without a family?

She'd known nothing but the institutional life of that little home. Raised in a group, sleeping in a row, eating in an assembly line. All her friends taken, one by one, forever to be replaced with other, younger babies. While she stayed. That was her life.

They are the only family she's ever known.

Long ago I'd asked for permission to adopt both Eden and Lily, and our agency wasn't close to considering it. It wouldn't have been fair, they said. Other families were waiting.

What families?

Two years ago, the agency had promised us they would care for her, assured us she would get a family, and had told us a year after that—wrongly—that she'd returned to her orphanage. Now it turned out they'd lost her right where they'd left her.

Our hearts broke.

. . . .

Something had gone wrong, obviously. Someone had made mistakes somewhere, or there had been some conflict. And something had transpired between the two agency offices to put the home office in the dark. We had no idea what. But one thing became clear very quickly: our inquiry was going to change everything. Whatever had frozen the file in the first place no longer mattered, and the forgotten file of a forgotten girl was now under lights.

"Match this child immediately." The CCCWA's command came swiftly.

My fingers flew over keys, continuing in email the conversation Rebecca and I had started on the phone. I had to stop typing to gather my thoughts. My mind was mash. What had I said to her on the phone, anyway? Too much? Enough? Anything? What in the world did this mean for us? And for that matter, what was I feeling? The news was so shocking I couldn't see my own mind. It took a conversation with Tammy to enable me to finish the email.

> Rebecca,
> We are so relieved that Liu Hai Rou is well. We still love her. She will always have a place in our hearts, no matter who her forever family becomes.
> But Tammy's first question was this: "Are they one hundred percent certain that the CCCWA would not let us adopt her?"
> I understand the rationale for everything you said on the phone. I understand the condition of placing her with a paperwork-ready family was theirs, not yours. When Liu Hai Rou is matched, we will be thrilled for both sides, and fully supportive.

114

But on the other hand, I could tell you stories of half a dozen times in the past two years that one of us, or both of us, sometimes at the same time or completely out of the blue, would bring Lily up, and have odd premonitions that someday a miracle would happen. I usually chalked it up to the effects of grief, and knew it was certainly out of our hands.

The fact is, Rebecca, Tammy's a wreck. You interact with adoptive mothers every day, I hope you can empathize.

Dann

This was the question *I* had: *Are YOU doing something, God?* All other questions would remain on hold as I sought the answer to that one.

I called a friend in town who'd adopted from China while living in China and who'd also run into complications. Their daughter had lived with them before they'd adopted her, and I learned on the phone call that during that time an adoption agency had matched their daughter-to-be with a different family. Our friends had searched for and found that family, who immediately understood the girl belonged with our friends. Together the families joined forces against a very displeased adoption agency and forced a CCCWA reassignment.

"If Lily's a Johnson in *his* eyes," my friend buoyed me, "she will no doubt also come home."

Don't give me such hope, God! Don't give it to me if it's not real.

Throughout the day I prayed. I wondered. I thought. I tried not to think. Later, back working at my desk, I broke down. Then I called another friend who had recently compiled a dossier while living in China. I needed to analyze how quickly we could compile our own.

I also called Sylvia in Beijing. She was extremely kind, and remembered everything that had happened with Lily. She told me she no longer worked for our agency. I shared what had just happened, and in her opinion, the agency was the key. If we could get the agency to relinquish the file, she believed the CCCWA would be completely fine with us adopting Liu Hai Rou directly through them. Nothing, she informed me, compelled expats to use an agency in the first place. She offered me the mobile phone number of her personal friend at the CCCWA. As exciting as that was, what I still cared about most was getting a handle on God's involvement. It didn't take wild imagining for things to look like he really might have been saving Lily for us.

Have you been saving her for us? Is she a Johnson in your eyes?

If I had those answers, nothing else would matter. I would do anything. But I didn't have them. God was silent.

Rebecca wrote back. Yes, they were one hundred percent sure we couldn't have her; yes, they'd neglected Liu Hai Rou's file for two plus years, then lost track of it, and then her; but no, waiting for us was not thinkable; no, it was not relevant we had a past match with the child; yes, they would be cramming this new adoption through immediately.

That's not how Rebecca wrote. She wrote kindly and tactfully. We just *felt* the "no" like brusque rejection. She tried to be encouraging by reminding us of how instrumental we had been in restoring Liu Hai Rou's health the first time around. She told us her hands were tied by the mandate from the CCCWA. Though she agreed: it was simple fact that a dossier-ready family could bring Liu Hai Rou home nine months earlier than we could, so that's what was best. "It's very important that we not hold up her placement any further."

You would advocate for her, to me?

By vocation, Rebecca advocated for orphans. It was natural she advocate for Lily.

But it felt like an affront. Of course waiting nine months to give her to us (and we had our doubts it would have to be that much longer) was more waiting time for Liu Hai Rou than giving her to another family immediately, but didn't that pale in comparison with the real tragedy?

Why aren't we speaking of the real tragedy?

This child, due to inexcusable behavior from whoever it had been, would, before it was all over, spend the first four years of her life without a family.

It could have been *one*.

It would affect her forever. She would never, ever get those years back.

I still had my CCCWA contact.

Listening to the woman's phone ring made my heart race—I had no idea what to expect on this call. I was taken aback by how exceedingly kind she was. She listened to my tale from start to finish as I labored through it in Chinese. At the end, I told her what would really help would be for her to read the email updates we'd written while we were losing Liu Hai Rou two years earlier.

She consented to me sending her those—yes, English would be fine. The next day I could not relax. It was heady stuff to have gone from thinking Lily was dead to less than twenty-four hours later talking on the phone with someone in the CCCWA.

I begged God for guidance. I asked again for a sign, kept reading the Word. Still nothing. I wanted to trust. I wanted to believe before I saw. I craved faith. The next day I walked to work the long way around, in disbelief over how this little girl could once again be at the center of the stretching of my deepest self. My heart broke to think Lily might have this one impact on my life— pain—and none other. I feared it. I longed for direction. I had no confidence I'd heard one word concerning what to do about her. Or one word about anything God was doing. I was in the dark, and it was killing me, and increasing my desperation for some kind of anything from above.

A faint thought put a moment's hitch in my step. *What...?*

Something, *wait...* It was... I saw... I had been...suppressing something.

Hope. I had been suppressing hope. From the first day, from the time I'd hung up the phone with Rebecca, I'd been subconsciously—but unmistakably, I could see it now—suppressing hope. I'd been afraid. I didn't want to hope. Not for Lily. Not again.

But as Hope had now bumped up against me hard enough to alert me it was there, I determined to beat it. I knew what it meant to hope and have everything crash to nothing. As long as there *wasn't* any hope—and there wasn't—it was best not to hope. Inquiring about possibilities with Lily's file was a far cry from getting my hopes up about her.

Then a real epiphany came. She was only a train ride away. I could go see her. Why not? The agency had their marching orders, but that didn't have to stop me. Why shouldn't I go and get some closure? That would be better than false hope, anyway.

My CCCWA contact emailed me back. She confirmed our worst fears. It was already too late. Our agency had matched Liu Hai Rou with someone else. There would be no reversing it. Grass had not grown under anyone's feet this time. Lily had a family. Because of us.

It moved me that this woman had condescended[33] to write me at all, and I was touched at her willingness to write me in my own language. She signed off by wishing us the best, then she added a postscript in the flowery beauty of her own mother tongue that

117

said, roughly translated, "My limited English does not give me the means to fully express the respect I feel for you and your wife. The story of your connection to Liu Hai Rou has moved me very deeply."

Her words were a silver lining on a very dark cloud.

What had failed to materialize in two years, we had catalyzed in two days. Delay would not be tolerated; it wouldn't be fair to the child. Fairness again. After all (and the inadvertent irony bit hard) why leave an orphaned child in foster care when there is a loving family who wants her?

If I was going to go to Beijing, now was the time. I tested the idea on Tammy on our date night. She didn't like it. But she let me talk, and the more she listened, the more she saw how important the trip had become for me. She let up, but said not to expect her to go. She did not need some road trip to figure out her feelings; she was barely holding herself together. Seeing Lily would be more than she could handle.

I would take the overnight train on Saturday.

I journaled in anticipation:

> Lord. Lily's gone from us. Again.
>
> It seems so inexplicable why it needed to be this way. It seems cruel. She could have already been adopted and we'd have been fine. But to have her still free after two years, and decide to go for her, only to—in two days—cause a match with someone else?
>
> Why?
>
> Why'd you have to do that to us?[34] I'm afraid it will always seem like grief-for-nothing unless you explain otherwise.

It was so strange to observe everywhere what looked like God's fingerprints, as if he were orchestrating the thing. Wouldn't Lily coming to us now be the most incredible miracle? But I couldn't go there. I had begged him at the beginning not to give me hope if it would turn out to be false hope. So to cling to it now? Impossible. I didn't mean hope in him, or trust in him, or confidence that he could do whatever he pleased. I meant hope that he would give us Lily. As to trust that *that* would come to pass, I had none.

Why should I?

All human reason was shouting, "It's over." Why should I

argue when I knew from the previous two days alone that doing so only made the pain worse.

I do not understand the connection I have with this child.

Because it resembled nothing common or normal for me otherwise.

And if it truly is from you, but I never discover the purpose of it, even though I ask, then what good is it? None. So I will never stop asking.

I wondered if I would ever stop loving her.

Will that be until I die? Or is the nearness of loss making me delusional?

My heart loudly complained that I wished God's orchestrating could be for a purpose that I liked. But it was safer to call the whole thing "cruel" and consider it over. Why entertain hope that his plan was to give her to us? She was headed for another family, and I had best force my thinking to align itself with that fact. This is what was going to happen. I hadn't heard God say anything different. It didn't matter how much we wanted her; I had no choice but to leave the mysteries well enough alone. Why we'd had to be involved. Why it had had to be so painful.

But I wasn't going to be able to stop asking "Why?" very easily.

Beijing Again

...to believe God for no other reason than, well...for
no reason at all? Can a person believe even when
God appears to him as an enemy?

Philip Yancey

MY TICKET WAS FOR 7:40.

In the morning, I would see Lily.

Breathe.

Much like in every adoption, I was a parent in love, traveling to
see my child for the first time. But unlike everyone else, I was not
matched with my child. I would go home the same way I went.
Alone.

I was only going so I could say goodbye.

> My Dearest Lily,
>
> I have done little else the past twelve hours other than think of
> writing you this letter. This morning I bought a train ticket. This
> evening I find myself lying in berth 26 of car 7 on the T44,
> service to Beijing. The morning will find me on my way to see
> you.
>
> You, of course, won't recognize me. You don't know who I am,
> as we've never seen each other. I wonder if you might even cry
> when you see me. Some kids who aren't used to foreigners do,
> you know, most notably my daughter Eden when we first met! If
> you cry, I won't take it personally.
>
> I very well may be crying myself.
>
> I've been crying a lot these past three days, sweetheart. That's

unusual for me, crying over sad things. In fact, it's only happened to me once before, and that story is about you, too. You see, we were supposed to have been your mommy and daddy. The only good part of that story was that you were brought to the home where you live now. I don't suppose you can even remember that you didn't always live there! You were born far away in another province, and, before turning one, got very, very sick. By the time you came to Beijing you had been vomiting for almost nine months. The move likely saved your life. The hope that it actually had was our sole comfort in those days of grief.

A few months later we were matched with the girl who became our daughter Eden. Before we met her, I was in Beijing and told our agency I wished we could add both of you girls to our family. They said it wouldn't be fair to other families who were waiting. But I couldn't help but ask. Love always hopes.

The part that was hard this week was finding out that you're still there. I don't know why, but we were told a year ago last summer that you had already gone back to your orphanage, your legal guardians, and the more months that went by, the more we assumed you had been adopted.

This week we wrote our former agency to ask if they knew where you were. Shock of all shocks, it came back that you'd never gone back, had never been put back in the system. It was almost too much to be believed. To think that for more than the entire time we have had Eden, for the whole two years of memories and bonds that we have been making with her—you've been there! Waiting.

Of course to you it hasn't felt like waiting—in fact you may be in for a bit of a rude awakening as your noodles and your chopsticks and your *baozi* and whatever else your favorites are and your aunties and your preschool friends all soon disappear! But don't worry, there will be many, many wonderful things too. Most important, a family. They want you! I learned only yesterday how very excited about you they are.

I know exactly how they feel.

It's just that it would have been so much better for you if it had happened two years ago.

Now we come to the difficult part.

Why were you left unadopted these two years? I very quickly began to question whether it could have possibly been something other than human error after all. *Could it be? Is it possible?*

121

Did God bring this about, human error merely a tool for his own purposes? I didn't dare ask, but I couldn't stop myself wondering, *Could his purpose have been to save her for us?* That, miracle of all unbelievable miracles, after all this time you would still be, like you were going to be before you got sick, becoming our daughter? I couldn't go there. My heart leapt at the mere hint of such fairy tale, yet the thought of such hope brought tears, and I shouted at God not to give it to me if it wasn't real.

And so the first time on the phone with our agency this week I merely asked "What if?" I didn't know myself whether I wanted to ask, "Can we have her?" I didn't know that Tammy (your mommy) already had.

My hesitation was *not at all* because I didn't know my heart, Lily. I knew my heart, because I have never stopped loving you. It doesn't seem I have a choice. I think I will love you for as long as I live, Lily. I know, sounds pretty strange coming from some guy you will see for the first time tomorrow morning! I don't even understand it myself. The only conclusion I can draw is that my Heavenly Father has put this father love for you in my heart. But sometimes—like right now—I really don't know why.

On that phone call, it wasn't love that kept me from asking. It was grief. We had lost you once, and I didn't want to lose you again. We were adjusted and acclimated and happy and fine with the idea that you were already part of another family—and we had joy in that because we love you. Then I learned that you were not adopted. But I couldn't say "We want her!" because I needed to think. I needed to come to some place of believing that amidst the paperwork and the craziness of it all there was some logical possibility, however thin, that the most amazing, crazy dream that we had talked about time and again might actually have a chance of becoming true. Or I needed assurance that God was doing this. If I had confidence in that, I wouldn't have worried a snit about paperwork or an agency or the CC-CWA or anything.

I've never doubted he could put you into our family if that's what he wanted. I've just never gotten to a place where I felt I knew that's what he was doing.

But now, to suddenly be faced with the reality that you were still available? That our family didn't need to be given special treatment, nor any other waiting family get unfair treatment? That you were just, other than two years older, the same as you were?

If the hand of God were in this, wouldn't it look just like this? I failed in my attempts to keep my mind from such thoughts. Nor was it the first time. I could tell you a half dozen stories from the past two years that looked like the hand of God. Whether they ever were or not we still don't know, and we never said we knew we would get you someday. We were just bewildered by how often it came up, sometimes by one of us, sometimes the other, once or twice by both of us at the same time.

I always assumed we must be wrong, and that there was a different wonderful family planned for you. And if that's what He wanted, then it was exactly what we wanted, too. What we were continuing to go through must be a natural part of the grieving process, we thought. But once in awhile we'd admit a "what if?" Other times I couldn't bring myself to do even that much. I especially could not bring myself to do it right after finding you still in Beijing.

It is possible for Hope to be too painful to mention aloud.

Then I made phone calls, each one more amazing than the last, until a mere twenty-four hours later I was talking with and exchanging personal emails with the CCCWA itself. It allowed me to dare consider again if it might not really be God after all.

I never did make that decision to "go for you again"—I simply realized at some point that I was.

And there would be no safety net. Hope came back. All the way and all by itself.

I was told on the phone this morning that your new family are wonderful people. I'm sure they are. I hope with all my heart they teach you to walk with Jesus. (You think my love is over the top!) But it is so sad to me that news about your new family, which two weeks ago would have been wonderful—tinged with wistfulness, sure—this same news gotten the day before yesterday has broken my heart.

I had forgotten how that feels.

The entire week of circumstances I am at a loss to understand. The most descriptive word I have settled on is: cruel. I know my pain is nothing compared to many. Of the myriad experiences afforded humanity, suffering is surely one of the ones I know the least about. But what exactly ended up being our role in this month's whole scenario? Drawing attention to your file. Precipitating in two days what had failed to take place in two years.

Everyone is in such a hurry to get you adopted now, and rightfully so—you're not a baby anymore, young lady! I understand this. It's just very difficult not to weigh in one hand the few extra months it might take for you to wait for us, and compare it in the other to the two years when no one did anything about you anyway. And who can say how long you would *still*, if not for us, be sitting there waiting?

Two years ago, we eventually became grateful for how we were used to get you out of your orphanage. Maybe someday I will also be grateful for being used to get you adopted out of Beijing. But right now, Princess, I am just sad. So very, very sad. Because now it is twice. Twice I have thought you would be ours, only to see you slip away.

That's why I'm coming to see you tomorrow, you know. To say goodbye. If I didn't come, I know I would regret it forever.

For the last time, I love you, Lily.

And so we come to a point of confession. Your name isn't really Lily. Up until now it's been Liu Hai Rou, but your new family will give you an English name that they will pick. It will become your real name. And they will love you as much as I do. And grow to love you more than I do because they will know the real you. And because of my respect for their love, I really can't ever give you this letter. It's addressed to you, but it's really for me. I had to write it to make progress toward understanding my own heart. So thank you for inspiring me; I will consider it kind of your last gift to me. It's been a privilege to love you, but at the same time overwhelming and scary to feel so much and not understand how. I know there are many more chapters of understanding to come. I am confident that someday I will see much more regarding what all of this has been about. But for now I am largely in the dark.

I will see you in the morning!

[I can't sign this.
I can't hear you call me anything but Daddy, but that's not me anymore.]

It had been four hours since I started writing, editing, and rewriting. At last, my heart had its bearings; I could close the computer. I'd found clarity. I knew how I felt. But I was wrung out, and my tear-drenched shirt needed to be. I walked down the swaying hall to the train bathroom and got ready for bed, then climbed back into my hard-sleeper top bunk. I fell asleep to the clack of wheels on rails, and heard nothing else before morning.

I did not arrive in Beijing without a plan. Again it had been Sylvia who extended kindness to me. The founders of the foster home were friends of hers, and the morning before my trip she had put me in contact with the wife, who had texted me an address. Not the foster home's, but a different place they went for Sunday morning church since I'd mentioned that's when I would be arriving. They'd said they'd bring the girl with them. I could meet her there.

It took two hours from the Beijing train station by bus, subway, and walking to reach the right apartment complex. I still got there before almost anyone else. I found the right building and took the most nerve-wracking elevator ride of my life. The woman who opened the apartment door introduced herself as the woman I'd talked with on the phone. I mentioned how long it had taken me to get there from the train station and she looked confused. Wasn't I popping in locally? I thought I'd told her where I lived, but now when I did, her confusion turned to shock. I saw a few faces behind her with similar reactions and realized I would be a curiosity indeed for having come so far to see this girl. I told my host how very kind she was for allowing me to come.

Where is she? I looked around.

"Come in, the girl is there in the back room, coloring pictures with the other kids. Go on back and see her."

I was glad she sent me instead of bringing me.

I could be alone with my thoughts.

I moved down the hall toward where she was.

I heard noise coming from the last room on the left.

I reached the open door.

Peeked inside.

Oh!

God, there she is…

Lily was at a small table, her seat facing the door. Her fine, straight hair was in pigtails, and she wore a coat. She looked older than I could believe. It wasn't that I didn't know her age, for I knew exactly how old she was—that day was her half-birthday. But the most recent pictures we had were from two years earlier, and mental pictures of children simply don't auto-update.

She was beautiful. It took me aback.

You are so…beautiful.

I took a few steps toward her.

That girl, that girl sitting there. That is Lily.

I'd never seen her. I had a hard time believing I was seeing her now. There she was. She was there.

Lily is real.

Moving. Breathing. I sat in the empty chair to her right. I looked at her fingernails, at a scratch on her hand, at her winter coat. It seemed impossible I had loved this girl—this girl I didn't know—as much as I had. I didn't understand.

How, Lord?

I craned my neck for a look at her left ear. As cute as ever. I didn't say anything, content to sit, crying and watching her color.

The room hushed, which made me notice that the half a dozen others in the room had been chatting and laughing up until that point. I glimpsed someone across the table elbow a younger co-worker, shushing her. Everyone watched me watch Lily. What explanation could I give? I knew they must have had some idea of who I was, but what man trains across China to look at an orphan? And what orphan, previously unmet, pulls tears down his cheeks by sitting there coloring? If it hadn't been happening to me, it wouldn't have made sense to me, either. I had no explanation.

Except for Lily, I didn't care about much else. Thrill over seeing her, intermixed with knowing it was likely the only time I ever would, stretched my heartstrings beyond all I'd known. All my life my head had ruled my heart. Now, in her presence, I was powerless to think at all. Feelings ruled. And they kept coming. I'd heard of running like a faucet, but I'd never had it happen to me before. I would for most of the rest of the day.

I took out a camera. So far, Lily hadn't so much as looked at me. But a camera proved too much to resist, and the video caught her shooting me a little dirty glance out of the corner of her eye. I laughed. It would not matter if I could make her like me or not. I would love it if I could, but I knew I was no one to her. I could say my goodbye and she didn't need to reciprocate anything.

It was time for the meeting to start, and I moved with the other adults to the main room. Dozens had arrived since I came in, so I squeezed into a seat in the second row, of about ten, from the back. The foster home lady was at the front leading singing. She had asked me ahead of time if I would share a few words as their guest, and while I would have loved to decline, I'd been in the culture long enough to know it was better if I didn't. I made the obligatory vague excuses about how poor my Chinese was, and I'd never been to one of these house meetings before, but they countered with praise of my language, and assurance that one of the leaders had good English, anyway. He could translate.

Some of the songs were familiar to me, and from my seat I plumbed depths that most of my life had not existed. And the paradox of worshiping Someone whom the day before I had accused of cruelty made me conflicted. Song after song pushed further tears—from deep places, secret places, doubting places, wounded places. I felt love, I felt pain.

The two feel…

They felt the furthest thing from opposites, that's what. I had trouble telling which was which. My love for Lily was pain. Pain had sprung to life because I loved her.

. . . .

Do you really love me?

Somewhere in adulthood I'd consciously questioned God on the matter for the first time. It was a heart cry, not a faith crisis.

I'd always known I was loved. The question was answered for child me as it is meant to be for all children, by parents. Their love was so certain I don't recall ever thinking about it. Adolescent me required the additional love of peers, though none of us used that word. People were labeled "cool" or "popular" or other things. We failed to recognize popularity as a poor substitute for real acceptance without condition. Adult me matured, and though I mastered the art of projecting an image of likability, I also came to know: real love is the kind with no strings attached.

Me? You love me? Not me as a part of humanity, but me, Dann. The guy. The man, the husband, the dad, the friend, the failure, the success?

Just me. You love me?

I hadn't asked him only once. Maybe my doubt was a result of coming to know myself better. Maybe it grew alongside a creeping dread about how little I'd accomplished with my life. Maybe it was early midlife crisis. Or maybe it was a heightened intellect, or a greater capacity for philosophizing, or for feeling. I didn't know. But it had become something I wondered about.

And that's what *kept* me wondering about it. People who know, really know—that they are loved—never think twice about it.

. . . .

The singing was still going on, though I was slowly wilting beneath speakers surely adequate for a space fifty times the size. I watched the passionate group of sincere brothers and sisters around me. I'd closed my eyes again to reflect on how close a bond I was feeling with them, when…so clearly and so startlingly that I thought I must have jolted (I opened an eye to check if anyone had noticed), a single sentence lit my mind.

The singing faded, irrelevant. The sentence I'd heard hadn't been an answer to the questions I'd been desperately asking that weekend. He did not tell me why this girl had not become ours. He did not tell me why I loved her so much. He said something else. He asked *me* a question.

> Do you think I could love you
> as much as you love her?

I was alone in the room.

Laid open. Nothing existed.

If I had been previously unsure whether or not I would at that moment care about such a question, the weight of it upon my soul shattered all doubt. It was decidedly not what I had been seeking that weekend, not even close, but it redirected every fiber of me like a laser onto something I'd been seeking all my life.

The question was not rhetorical.

It awaited my reply.

The answer came as clearly as the question had. Only I delayed relaying it, thinking to hold out and think of something better.

No dice.

No, I don't guess I believe that you do.

How could I? How could I possibly believe that? I was dying here. I'd never loved anything so painfully in all my life. I was helpless. Desperate. Out of my depth. Flailing. What possible resemblance could my love for her bear to God's love for me? I was floundering and lost, had never known that either love or pain could descend so deep. And I was supposed to have formed some link between all that and what role feelings played in the love of a sovereign God?

128

It hit me, though, and oddly so because I'd never thought about it, that my feelings that day, so overwhelmingly inscrutable to me, were perfectly understood by him. He'd created my capacity to feel them. It was like a door, onto God or into heaven, cracked open. What little I glimpsed through was too much for me.

How little I must understand.

Had ever understood. Ever known. To ponder what I still must lack was almost frightening.

How much deeper do life and love and pain go? How deep will THIS go?

Before Lily, I'd had little reason to think I had anything to learn about pain. My own wife in the pain of infertility had not uprooted my ignorant self-assurance. It had taken Lily. In losing her I learned what pain was. Now I was losing her again. And God was asking if I knew what love was.

No, I don't guess I believe that you do.

Apparently I had no real idea what "he loves me" meant.

Goodbye, My Dearest

I can't see how You're leading me unless You've led me here
Where I'm lost enough to let myself be led
And so You've been here all along I guess
It's just Your ways and You are just plain hard to get

Rich Mullins, "Hard to Get"

THEY'D SAVED MY SHARING for last. My eyes had dried while the leader talked, but as soon as I was standing up front, the faucet strained toward "on" again. I got no further than telling them why I was there, then all was silent as they waited for me to collect myself. I turned to my translator and said I would speak Chinese until I needed him to rescue me. My voice started up again, but to this day I do not remember what I said to those people. Whatever it was, I'd forgotten most of it before I'd even left the room. I spoke of the little girl in the back room and the love for her that was consuming me. Deep inner feelings tumbled out without filter, and I shared straight from the yawning hole of a broken heart. Nothing felt more important than declaring my love for her.

Just before wrapping up, I remembered my translator for the first time. The image of his blank face and wide eyes burned itself into forever memory, and was perhaps what drove my own words out from the same. I picked my way back to my seat and fumbled for a mental drawer in which to comfortably file "spontaneous public blathering." I had none. For months I would cringe any time I recalled the event. God may, of course, use anyone he chooses, even (especially?) those willing to play the fool, but having been the fool that morning gave me little pleasure afterwards. My only comfort lay in knowing I would never have to see those people again.

The service ended. I thought only of Lily. The foster home woman told me I would be sharing a taxi with the two caregivers taking her back to the home. When the four of us were ready, we left. Lily walked between me and one of them, grabbing our hands and asking us to swing her by her arms. I pinched myself. We passed some of the complex's playground equipment, and she ran to climb on it. The other girl called to her to come back.

It brought me up short.

What did she just call her?

It wasn't her name. It wasn't a derivative or shortening of it, either. She'd said not one character from Liu Hai Rou. In fact, if I'd heard right, she hadn't even called her a girl's name. She'd said a man's name.

"Wait a minute, what did you just call her?"

"Enoch."

"Enoch! Why Enoch? That's a boy's name."

One brief paragraph in Genesis chapter 5 contains the written record of the man Enoch. He walked with God and was no more. He did not taste death, for God took him. It had been ten years since we'd stumbled on the name in my Norwegian lineage and given it to our firstborn.

Now I learned that for her entire Beijing life, it had been Lily's name, too.

"Isn't that kind of strange to name a girl Enoch? How'd she come to be called that?"

"I don't know, really. She was very sick when we got her, and when she started to get well... I guess they named her because of that. She didn't die."

. . . .

The taxi ride took an hour, and from the front seat I played peek-a-boo with Lily in the back. Her laughs and giggles were surreal. Though it felt good to build some rapport with her, I couldn't really feel all that good about it. Her over-ease with strangers was common in children whose attachments had not been normal, or adequate.

Nap time was half over by the time we arrived, so the workers quickly fed Lily and laid her down in the main room. The other children were asleep in their beds upstairs. I wasn't hungry, and not about to make a trip out and sacrifice time near Lily over something so pedestrian as eating. Instead I found myself a spot on the far side of the room and lay down on the tile floor covered over with China's ubiquitous foam puzzle squares. As I gazed around at the walls and the row of high chairs along one of them, I wondered why everything looked so familiar. Of course! This was the room where the videos Ivy gave me had been taken. The same week I'd been to the agency office during our match with Eden. Lily had been here. She was still here. What percentage of her waking life had been spent in this very room where we now lay? Seventy? Eighty, ninety?

God…

She wasn't sleeping. The workers told her she could get up. She went to get a book and wanted me to read to her. While the workers busied themselves in the kitchen, Lily plopped herself in my lap. I froze.

Lily, our Lily, was sitting in my lap.

I read her the book.

Self, you should kiss her.

Could I?

A man kisses his own kids, perhaps might peck the head of a niece or nephew, but kissing is not a normal sign of affection with even the children of very close friends. At least not in my culture. Other cultures might kiss with every hello. But some conventions —China's, for instance—run in the opposite direction. I couldn't recall observing someone kiss even his own child.

You should kiss her.

There was no one else to do it. Not one person in the whole world loved this child more than Tammy and I did. I was here to say goodbye, and doggone it, Lily was going to get a goodbye kiss.

I planted one on the top of her head. She leafed through the book again. I gave her a peck on the right cheek. She kept reading, sucking a lollipop loudly.

"I love you, Lily."

Finally, I turned her head and kissed the cute little left ear that had captured me at the very beginning.

"I know, Lily. I'm a glassy-eyed stranger sitting here holding you and giving you goodbye kisses. But I have loved you since before you can remember, what do you think of that?"

She sucked her lollipop still louder, and watched me talking to her in English. Then she switched the lollipop into the other cheek and hopped up to get another book. I stared as she came back with a thick photo album. Pictures of her. I gobbled them up as she turned the pages for me.

Some family will be lucky indeed to be handed this.

Lily loved looking at her own pictures. In the first few pages she wasn't terribly older than when she had been matched with us, though there was some gap, for no photos had been included until she had put on some weight. Some of the pictures were only of her, others were taken with friends. I pointed at her in one of these and asked, "Who's this?"

"Enoch!" she shouted.

I did it again, and she shouted and laughed again, louder, then rushed to find herself in the next one. The longer we did it the harder she laughed. I noticed she had no problem pronouncing her name, for in Chinese it has only vowels and a nasal consonant. I asked if she could show me the back of her throat, and I saw she'd had her cleft soft palate repaired. It was uncanny how similar her Mandarin sounded to Eden's consonant-less English. Clear speech for both of them would take time, probably therapy.

All of a sudden a crew stood in the doorway. The kids were up from nap, and the atmosphere changed drastically. Babies were strapped in high chairs for a snack. Older children began playing. Volunteers showed up to spend their Sunday afternoon playing with them. The toys were all gotten out. Essentially, for China, it was a model foster home. Even the founding couple showed up to play, and clearly it was not a rare occurrence, for all the kids adored them. At first I preferred to stay sitting along the wall watching Lily, but eventually I got up to play with the babies and wrestle with some of the boys.

I talked to one volunteer named May, a Chinese woman who'd lived in the States for decades. When I told her why I had come, she said she'd been there when Liu Hai Rou first arrived. I'd never imagined hearing the story, let alone from someone speaking fluent English. The story of what had happened to Lily after they re-scinded the match was largely a blank for us. I sat mesmerized while May unfolded it for me.

Enoch (all May had ever called her) had been flown from her home province to be housed in this foster home while undergoing medical evaluation. Upon her arrival she had been skin and bones, with no meat on her anywhere. None of the workers had ever seen a child in such bad condition. Her spine protruded so much it *felt* like spines if you ran your hand along it. They doubted she had ever in her life ingested anything but liquids. Someone wondered aloud if they were looking at a body ravaged by AIDS. She looked like she might just as soon die as live.

At the hospital, doctors couldn't diagnose her. And so the entire foster home began to pray over her. Repeatedly they gathered and prayed. They prayed for healing and restoration and life, and they did not stop until the threat of death receded. To introduce food, they started with one Cheerio at a time and manually worked her jaw open and closed to melt it. Over time, she began to chew them herself. The vomiting ceased. Then her dysfunctions with taste, touch, hearing, and smell surfaced. Her sensory issues were off the charts. She was drastically underdeveloped. She could sit up but not stand. She had poor hand-eye coordination. She could do almost nothing other children her age could do. May, along with other volunteers, came day after day, week after week, and worked tirelessly with Enoch, moving her forward step by step, touching her, massaging her, loving her.

Tammy and I had had no idea Lily had been in such hands. No one had shared with us the miracles of her recovery. May's role in saving Lily had been as invaluable as ours had been, and through my tears I thanked her and blessed her for everything she'd done.

And together we watched this streak of lightning commandeer the playroom. I beheld with new eyes the shrieking miracle before me, the cutest thing in the room. Suddenly, she left; I followed her out to see where she'd go. She went to the hall bathroom, got out a stool, turned on the water, used soap, washed her hands, dried them, and switched off the light. All by herself. So independent. It may have been skillful, but I didn't think it was cute, impressive, or praiseworthy. I saw only the unattached and broken child within, and it made me sad. She should have had a family so long ago.

Out in the main room again, the lead couple invited me to an early supper, but I declined. I insisted I was not hungry. I went for a short walk instead, hoping they would leave in my absence. On my return, I was relieved to see that they had. I was free to watch Lily play again. My minutes were precious and few, now. The day was ending. But to my horror the couple came back, and this time their invitation to dinner was insistent. They had their agenda, and did not understand mine. I didn't want to go, but I'd been pushing it the first time. Further rudeness would turn my visit to trespass. I was unendingly grateful that they had welcomed my coming, but I could hardly convey my current feelings—"I'm not here to talk with you"—to their faces.

But I had to go.

Dinner was awkward, due in no small part to my attitude. I ached the entire time to get back to Lily.

What am I missing? What is her evening routine like?

By the time the meal ended, it had grown dark outside. Our party of four (they'd brought along one of the workers) walked back to the home to find everything quiet, the living room empty, and the workers resting. They told me the kids had gone to bed.

I would rather they'd have stuck me with the kitchen knife. I had missed everything.

The husband, already up the stairs, was saying good-night to the kids who were still awake, and they told me I could follow him up. I found him stepping between rooms, and he indicated the one Lily was in. I found her by the light of my phone in the second crib in a row of seven. My light shone onto the peaceful face of a child sound asleep. I was crestfallen. I had come to say goodbye and been robbed of my chance to do it.

The guy joined me, and a flare of anger lit my chest. I was even more ticked at myself. I'd allowed myself to be taken away to a dinner I did not want to attend, to eat with people I did not want to get to know, and in so doing I'd sacrificed my last two precious hours with Lily.

What is wrong with you?

I waited for him to leave so I could at least have a moment to gather my thoughts and end the day in peace instead of turmoil. There was one last thing I could still do: pray over her while she slept.

The silence got long and I realized he wasn't leaving. He was waiting for me to leave.

"Would it be okay if I had just a moment alone with her?"

"Not okay." His offhanded rebuff was jarring.

"I just want to say a prayer for her, say goodbye."

"We'll pray for her together."

My closed teeth formed a smile, "After you."

I didn't listen to his prayer. I prayed my own, venting my anger at the ruination of my special day.

God suggested some alternative views of the man, but I

pushed them aside. I did not want to see a good man, or a brother, or a rare champion, a male champion no less, for the orphan in China. I had only anger. (I'd never had to make an effort for feeling that one.) At the same time, I hated my own pettiness. Why couldn't I pretend he wasn't there and just enjoy these final moments? Inner turmoil crippled me.

By the time he was finished, I had calmed enough to get a deep breath, in which I repented. I thanked God that holiness didn't emanate from the crosses I did or didn't take up, but from the one that Someone else had taken up for me. Then I prayed for Lily.

I thanked him for the gift of that little life sleeping before me in the light of two cell phones. I thanked him for saving her from death long ago, and I thanked him for the unbelievable privilege it had been to meet her and spend a day with her. I told him I did not understand what was going on in my heart, and that I could not comprehend the depths of love he had given me for her. I told him I was bewildered and deeply hurt she was being taken from us a second time. And especially that it had been our inquiry that had initiated it. Again I pledged my loyalty to him, which would never be based on circumstance. I begged him to speak, to guide, and to let me know that he saw. And cared. And knew all that was transpiring in my muddled, aching, broken heart.

"Lastly, God, bless this little girl. Lead her to know how much you love her."

With my amen, I turned to go, releasing Liu Hai Rou to live life as she always had. Without me.

The Bravest Thing of All

And up against this starry sea
I thought that you were meant for me.
I thought that you were meant for me.

Brave Saint Saturn, "Binary"

I RAN FROM THE room and down the stairs, aching to feel the moment instead of my anger. I had to leave. The experience was over.

Downstairs, I thanked all the workers I'd spent the day with. The one who'd been at the coloring table in the morning was the one who had gone to supper with us. Her eyes were wet; all day she had seemed to understand. I thanked the wife for her permission to visit, and I thanked the husband, who by now had also come downstairs.

The latest trains had departed, so I would fly home the next day. I needed a hotel. The husband accompanied me out of the neighborhood to a place where I could get a taxi. As we walked, I knew he'd done nothing wrong at the crib. In fact, he'd done exactly what he should have done, what I would have done in his place. Seeing it now only made me feel foolish, and I was more agitated than ever to clear out. I wished I could break into a run.

Our goodbye at the taxi stand was all smiles and politeness, and I regretted having thought of him so uncharitably. He did not deserve it. After directing my taxi driver to my hotel, I collapsed back against my seat, suddenly wondering what a soldier feels like when he comes back from war.

At the hotel business office I bought a ticket for the first flight out. Then I got a room, took myself and no luggage upstairs, and admitted I was curious to see what emotions would course through me now that I was alone again.

None.

I took my time showering, getting ready for bed, and went on feeling nothing. Just as an experiment, I *tried* to call up the feelings that had been ruling me a few hours earlier. I couldn't. Couldn't feel them. That guy was gone. I had no tears left.

After getting under the covers, I called Tammy to tell her I hadn't gotten a train or flight and would be home the next day.

"Are you glad you went?"

"Absolutely, completely and totally. I wouldn't have missed it."

As we talked, I could feel her own resistance diminishing. "Do you really think I could do it, too?"

I did. Sure, it was emotional, but there was this one narrow window and that was it. See Lily now or see her never. I encouraged her to pray about it some more.

Tammy was less surprised than I at my blank emotions. But after the day I'd just had, I couldn't get my head around how little, how normal, I was feeling. Maybe the trip had been the closure I'd needed.

"Maybe it's over for me, dear."

Lily would be adopted, and I would be happy for her.

We hung up. Used to rock-hard Chinese hotel beds, I slept like a baby.

I woke early the next morning and got out the door with oodles of time to catch the first train to the airport. I wasn't about to repeat my airport train debacle from the year before. Once on board, I made sure to limit my diversions to looking out the window—no books. Rows of dusty-looking poplar trees flew by in the pre-dawn light. As the mist gave way to brighter gray, I caught a glimpse of the apartment complex half a mile off where we'd lived for the final two months of Tammy's pregnancy with Elijah. Then, adjacent to the tracks, the park where we'd flown kites. More forlorn trees, towering among dunes of their own dusty leaves. I wondered how many weren't from this year, and had been there last autumn when I'd ridden by reading my book.

I wonder how many are from the year before that? When she came to live here.

Would everything make me think of her?

It would be a relief having it over.

138

At the airport I detrained like a pro, checked in, sailed security, and boarded my flight. Middle seats on full flights call for headphones and a resolve not to accidentally speak any Chinese. I am seldom chatty, but that day felt downright hermitic. The plane backed from the gate on schedule, and just before accelerating for takeoff, I thought I might just say it one last time. Inside my head.

Goodbye, Lily.

And a tidal wave crushed me. If possible, more violently than at any point the previous day.

The hotel room would have been a whole lot more convenient place for this than the middle of economy, Dann.

All I could do was ignore my fellow passengers and keep my spurting eyes closed. Clearly, just because I couldn't call up feelings at will did not indicate they no longer existed. That had been a serious miscalculation, but how was I to know? The world of feelings wasn't my world. Now they'd all leapt out of hiding, and I was spinning. I dialed up a worship playlist and turned inwards. Four variations in a row of "How Deep the Father's Love for Us"[35] played to my soul.

Do you know, God, really know, what this feels like for me? Do YOU feel feelings? Aching, longing feelings like these? About people? About me? I am losing a daughter—what was it like for you when you lost your Son?

Another feeling whooshed in to take a place alongside the rest. Gratitude. My ache to be dad to Lily was shining new light on my own Heavenly Dad. I was his. He was mine.

Joy held hands with Agony.

God, what are you up to? Can you not tell me? Can you not let me know what is going to happen to us? To her?

I only half-asked. It was beginning to dawn on me that the questions at the tops of my lists did not often correspond to the answers at the tops of his.

A few more songs played and my chest did the short, stuttering intake of breaths that always makes me nostalgic for a just-passed good cry from childhood. I needed some more deep breathing. I needed an emotional break. I scrolled through my phone for something else to listen to. My eye caught the albums Yao Shu Ting had listened to on the bus. Carelessly I clicked on a track with a good tune. I wanted to think about something other than Lily for awhile, or even better, nothing at all.

Only to land on lyrics that turned bonfire to forest fire. Doomed hope. Lostness. Haunted dreams. Goodbyes.

I staggered helplessly, as possible as that is in the middle seat in economy. Yet the screws only tightened further as the random feature next torturously selected a spoken monologue which I often skipped over. It finished me off:

> Have you given up yet?
> What hope lingers in the crevasses and corners of your soul?
> I know you
> You haven't given up yet…
> Sometimes the bravest thing of all is to hope.[36]

I was choking.
God?
A one-two punch, total knockout.
Really?
I saw it clearly, though. I hoped. I was hoping. I hoped that Lily would still become ours.
But why?
I hadn't consciously known I was still hoping until that moment. But already it was past tense. Hope had happened to me.
But oh, man, God, why? What could be more pointless?
Hope had chosen me.
I could reject it. Or I could embrace it. Embrace hope when there was none. It was surely pointless.
Sometimes the bravest thing of all is to hope.
The past day and a half had been brutal. Hope promised to stretch that torment over months. I didn't think I *was* that brave. To choose hope was to choose suffering.
But I wasn't choosing. She was my daughter. Hope was my destiny.

. . . .

One great result from my trip was how much more I fell in love with Eden. I could so much more easily imagine her orphanage days, picture her crying all alone, and feel the loss of all that she had missed out on in the first year of life. She became more precious, more cute, and I was never more sure I wouldn't have traded her for the world. Or Lily.
Were we waiting for God to do a miracle—I often daydreamed

what that could look like—or would we only get our answer once her adoption had run its course? Some days hope would rise, like the morning I read: "The Lord longs to be gracious to you; he rises to show you compassion, for the Lord is a God of justice. Blessed are all who wait for Him!" (Isaiah 30:18).

Other days were different:

> … adrift, depressed, unmotivated, leaderless, directionless, apathetic mixed with irritable, confused, needy, homesick, job-sick, lacking purpose… any more? I don't know what I'm feeling, or why. How much the Lily situation affects everything else, I don't even know. Much of last week I felt like a dried-out washcloth. Wrung out and left.

I had no idea when feelings would come or go, but mostly they went. Each passing day pushed the intensity of my trip further to the background. The emotionally heightened man who'd gone to Beijing was a stranger I couldn't relate to. Defeated thoughts came far more readily than hopeful ones:

Wouldn't it be better to lose her for good rather than endure this unending unknown?

Already, I wasn't even sure if losing her would hurt any more.

Tammy, experiencing the identical events, went through struggles colored by who she was, struggles very different from mine. But we had one similarity. She, though by a different road, had come to the same place of hope. At least that aspect of our future stretched before us clearly, though it offered no promises about how things would end. Tammy, too, was aware that choosing hope meant more pain in the end if it all came to nothing.

As the rawness receded, resentment replaced it. Yes, it was less convenient, less efficient, and far more messy to live emotionally, but I didn't prefer stoicism. The absence of emotion felt less… alive. I had tasted a fuller life, a more abundant[37] life, and it was gift. I didn't mean I wanted to hurt again, but I did mean that as long as things existed for which hurt was a natural response, hurting was better than feeling nothing.

Mommy's Trip

Does any human emotion run as deep as hope?

Philip Yancey

TAMMY COULD NOT DECIDE whether to go to Beijing to see Lily or not. She didn't know if it would help bring closure or only make things worse. She wanted her own chance at saying goodbye, but worried it might not turn out like she hoped. She decided she would only go if something dropped in her lap. A week after my trip her phone rang. Our current intern's mom and grandmother were coming from Iowa to visit her. They wanted to see Beijing first; would Tammy be willing to bring their (grand)daughter to meet their flight and take them all sightseeing? They would pay her way.

Lily, here comes your mom.

When the day came for their trip, Tammy was a bundle of nerves. She headed off to the airport with a heart-fire raging out of control, and she hated it. Late that night, once she was tucked in a hotel bed, I got a text informing me they'd arrived. The desk clerk had been named Lily.

The adventure had begun.

Tammy didn't know whether that check-in coincidence felt like kindness, a cruel joke, a test, or all of the above. She admitted the enlargement of her heart via pain had to be a good thing, but that was a far cry from wanting it. The pain hurt. The unfairness of Lily's new match made her want to lash out and fight. She knew the pain would probably lead to a deeper walk with God, but to be honest she just wanted Lily. Her inner conflict tossed her first one

142

way, then another, taunting her, calling her selfish. Immature.

> I do not know why we've been reconnected with Lily, but I will trust you. Forgive me for my lack of faith, forgive me for allowing this fire to make me angry and faithless.
> I need you. I need you to hold on to me and walk with me through it. I will not give up hope, for to reject hope now would be like rejecting you. No, I will allow my heart to hope, to hurt, and to trust. I praise you not for what I see, but for all I can't see. I praise you not for what I get, but for who you are.
> My heart cannot comprehend the love that would ask a beloved son to suffer and die so that other children could be adopted. How dare I ever whine or question your love. Please be patient with me and lead me gently through this.
> Thank you so much for Eden—this pain has reminded me what a gift she is. You have redeemed her life. You have shown us your father heart through her.
> Thank you for calling us to walk this road. There is nothing and no one I desire more than you, so if living this strange drama and walking this heart-risking path means I will be closer to you and know you more deeply—then lead on.

After a long, circuitous taxi ride with a driver who refused to listen to directions, Tammy and the intern did not arrive at Lily's foster home until mid-afternoon. That morning they'd attended the large international fellowship in town, and the first song sung had been a chorus about God moving mountains. Tear tracks were all that accompanied Tammy's silence as the auditorium filled with voices. Nothing would be greater than God moving the mountain that stood between her and Lily. But reality mocked the hope she'd chosen.

After their arrival at the children's home, they were invited in, and Lily was the first kid Tammy saw, standing in the kitchen doorway. But all the other kids swamped her and kept her from crossing the room. Everyone clamored for attention. Except Lily. She inexplicably stayed aloof and seemed to want nothing to do with Tammy. Only when Tammy got out her camera to take pictures of the kids and show them their faces did Lily come over to join in. Then she not only started wanting Tammy, she wanted to monopolize her and keep her for herself.

The two of them sat together and ate a snack side by side. Lily held her popcorn in one hand and Tammy's hand with the other. Then she got up to play, and Tammy watched, like I had. After a while Tammy got up and played, too. Next, all the kids Lily's age put on a performance. They had songs they'd memorized and motions to go with them. Tammy's camera captured every adorable second.

When the show was over, Tammy pulled out a special bag of wrapped goodies she'd prepared at home: little rubber bouncy balls with flashing lights, small games, and puzzles. There were enough for every child to unwrap one. Lily got the best gift of all, or at least she thought so: a little plastic princess wand that lit up and played music. Around and around the room she waltzed—singing, dancing, and waving the wand. Every inch the Princess she was born to be.

A boy saw a toy up on a high shelf that he wanted. He came and tugged on Tammy's shirt for her to get it for him. She got up, and Lily shadowed her. But when Tammy reached the one toy it bumped another one, which rolled, fell, and landed squarely on Lily's upturned face. Tammy was horrified. Blood started spurting. She scooped up Lily and went in search of a cloth. She applied pressure to a small cut over Lily's eye and a gash near her nose. The helpers brought them to a side room where they cleaned Lily's cuts and put an adhesive bandage on her nose. Tammy persuaded them not to put one on the small eye cut as it had stopped bleeding, and Lily's file said she was allergic to latex.

Lily clung to Tammy. She refused even her favorite helper. It ripped Tammy's mama heart apart to be wanted by her precious girl like that. How long had she loved this child? Finding her after two years, only to have her now in her arms, not wanting to let go, pierced her excruciatingly. It made no sense, though, because Lily liked her helpers, and some of them she'd known most of her life. Why was she clinging to a stranger? What was going on in that little soul to make her desperate for Tammy when she was hurt? Tammy couldn't guess. Long would it haunt her.

She didn't want to let go of Lily any more than Lily wanted to let go of her. But she would have to; protocol dictated that the workers take Lily to the clinic for a penicillin shot. In a minute Lily would be out the door. And out of reach.

> After I got Lily to let go of me enough for us to get her coat on, I quickly prayed for her then kissed her on the cheek. And then

144

they took her. My heart was so anxious from the stress of the accident that I couldn't feel anything about the parting. We left for the airport shortly after. My heartbeat only calmed down hours later once I reached the helper by phone, and she told me Enoch (Lily) was fine.

I had wanted my final moments with her to feel like I was assuring her of her new family's love. I wanted them to feel like goodbye.

They didn't. I watched her go and refused to believe it was the last time I'd see her. I refused to say the word goodbye. In fact, to Dann I said different words. Very different words.

Father, I do not know what you are doing. Have your way. I trust you no matter what.

The words she'd said to me had come via two text messages during the visit.

"This girl would so fit in our family."

"Dann, I want her!"

Nothing Happens...While Everything Happens

If hope springs eternal it never does here
I guess I lost all my hope last year
I tried to steal the moon from the sky
I am lost and lonely
I drift in space
My dreams are haunted by her face

Brave Saint Saturn, "Binary"

TAMMY WAS HOME, AND life went on. Nothing changed. We heard no news. I stopped mentioning Lily in my journal.

Our family celebrated Christmas and thoughts of Lily were pushed aside. I felt like months had passed since we'd talked about her, only to be brought up short one day as I calculated Tammy's trip had been less than three weeks prior.

I was pricked again picking up the Psalms. One began, "Do not be afraid," and as soon as I read it, I knew.

I was afraid.

Afraid of losing her forever.

There would be nothing I could do to fight it. Not this time. I wasn't in control. The ball was in God's court. It was not his ability I doubted, only his intention. I could find no faith to tell me he would give us what we wanted.

When the new year came, we went to Thailand. Every year before Chinese New Year we got to count down the days for gray, smoggy cold to be replaced with sunny seaside warmth. Totally spoiled. Vacationing in a destination that for North Americans is often reserved for the privileged was a blessing we never took for granted. Thailand wasn't quite the same eat-drink-snorkel-scuba-dive-and-lounge-on-endless-white-beaches-for-dollars-a-day destination we'd visited in our pre-children days, but it was still affordable, and still one of our all-time favorite places.

And not only did we get to vacation at the beach, we got to go to the dentist. And the ENT.[38] And get shots. And do cleft palate surgeries. Bangkok's medical facilities are world class and don't cost an arm and a leg, double amputations excepted. We generally made around two dozen medical appointments every year. Then, once those were out of the way, we made great vacation memories together.

That particular year turned out to be one of our most memorable Thailand trips ever. For starters, I got a surprise nose job. For years I'd suffered from sinus problems,[39] but that year my ENT ordered an MRI and told me afterwards he didn't know how I was breathing at all. Frankly, I wasn't. Not through my nose. I had to take breaks when eating just so I could suck in air.

"You need surgery."

Wow, that hadn't been my plan, but the evidence was compelling. As it turned out, I needed two: rhinoplasty on my septum and an endoscopic procedure for clearing out polyps. As a bonus, Tammy's birthday was the only available surgery day. So, coming to see me in recovery, she got to celebrate turning thirty-nine with a ninety-minute taxi ride with four children across steamy Bangkok.

Taxi rides are never steamy in Bangkok, no matter how hot it gets. But she managed to flag down the one taxi in town without air conditioning, which meant cruising with four open smell portals as well. Then the driver got lost.

Taxi rides to that hospital are never ninety minutes, either. We'd made it in fifteen. In bad traffic it might be an hour. But he drove and drove until Tammy wondered if they'd left Bangkok. Finally they pulled in. At first Tammy freaked. Why all the military? Had that year's protests come to the hospital? Then she realized it was a military hospital. Why on earth had the driver thought they wanted to come to this hospital? One more time she repeated the name of my hospital and crossed her fingers as the driver pulled back into the street.

The day was fast becoming her worst birthday ever. Just then, so appropriately, came the icing on the cake. Poor car-sick-prone Elijah vomited all over the back seat. And himself. And mom. The rest of the kids grumbled it had been steamy and smelly enough back there.

Eventually my family lurched into my hospital room. I wasn't there. I was supposed to have been out of surgery for two hours already. Tammy's birthday luck didn't improve as she could only find nurses who didn't speak English, so no explanations were forthcoming. Had something gone wrong? Why was her husband not out of surgery? The panicked nausea that accompanied these thoughts jogged Tammy's mind to the substance drying on the front of her shirt, and she dashed to the bathroom with Elijah to clean up.

When they finally wheeled me into my room in a post-surgery stupor, my family had gone to eat, and I didn't know they'd been there. I was still blurring in and out of consciousness, harassed by this on-again-off-again memory that I'd been crying in the recovery room. By the time they strolled in with their fast food leftovers, I felt much better. But I must not have looked it, for Tammy took one look and had to avert her eyes lest *she* pull an Elijah. The few remaining family members who didn't feel sick consumed the food they'd brought for celebrating, and with that, it was time to go. The favored birthday girl was anxious to leave before rush hour started.

I spent two days in recovery, and loved every minute. The hours of quiet were rarity itself. I enjoyed them so much I used my free hospital wifi to research optional surgeries I might schedule for the next year. I read and slept and ate Au Bon Pain. I had to enforce a strict limit for myself when it came to their pecan rolls. Three per day, max. Except special days. I proceeded to declare all hospital recovery days special.

I also had far too much time for thinking about Lily.

At some point, and I later blamed the two 15-foot sponges shoved up my nostrils and compressing my brain, I decided it was a bright idea to write Rebecca and ask for an update. Liu Hai Rou's matched family was none of our business, but I felt desperate for any kind of news. The constant swirling of wild speculation in my head over how Lily might conceivably come to us was driving me mad. We'd heard nothing in two months. There was no reason to think the situation had changed, but what if it had? What if the match had ended for some reason? I wasn't hoping anything bad had happened to the family she'd been matched with; perhaps there'd been a good thing. Maybe they'd gotten pregnant.[40] How was I to know?

My theorizing was becoming unbearable.

This time around I wasn't trying to persuade Rebecca of anything, I wasn't sharing what we were thinking or feeling, and there was nothing to argue about. In fact, I'd become persuaded that God had said—if he were going to do this thing—he didn't need my help. It embarrassed me to pester Rebecca about the other family, but, at least in my hospital bed stupor, I thought I might just hint around for a tidbit of information. What other choice did I have when we had chosen hope? A scrap of news, and maybe we'd feel some kind of direction about how to go on.

Rebecca answered everything in my email but the question I cared about. This was even more embarrassing than asking had been, since I was fully recovered by the time she replied.

With our medical appointments completed, we made our way to the beach. We found a great new restaurant on the second day. Eating there was a treat, every dish both beautiful and delicious, even by Thai standards. But finding it would prove memorable for more than the food. The husband, the artist in the kitchen, was also an artist on canvas. As his wife helped us push three tables together, the display of his oil paintings along one wall caught my eye. The world stopped.

A water lily.

Tammy finished putting in a quick order, and I turned from staring at that painting back to the table. I said grace.

"Heavenly Father, thank you for food. Thank you for fam…" I couldn't get any more out. A lump the size of my heart, or maybe it was my heart, blocked my throat.

I looked at Tammy. Her tears mirrored mine—she'd seen it, too.

It's the only painting we've ever bought. It would travel home to China to be matted and framed and hung in our living room. It hangs there still.

When rolling it up and paying for it after supper, I tried to explain to the wife why we liked her husband's painting so much. It turned out her English did not extend all that far beyond the menu, but she did understand me say "lily."

"No," she corrected me, "not lily. Is lotus." Shoot, Thailand, I should have known.

Now I felt stupid for my impulsiveness, but it wasn't like I could hand the thing back. Then I *was* stupid and failed to avail myself of a dictionary and learn that a lotus *is* a lily, a type of large water lily. Instead I had a little pity party, and only came out of it when I hit on this way to make myself feel better:

It's even more appropriate we bought a painting that only seems to be a lily, but isn't. Because neither is she.

My floral ignorance aside, the reaction I'd had to the painting shook me. What was happening to me? I didn't have the first clue what to do with the power this girl held over me. An allusion to her name had just moved me more than I was accustomed to being moved by anything.

Never had life been like this. I walked a knife-edge, lived at a breaking point. Were we waiting for something or weren't we? The entire odyssey assaulted me without end. I failed to recognize life; every day was mystery. Even the mundane seemed pregnant with significance. The tension between hope and hopelessness ratcheted tighter.

But no news came.

. . . .

Back home in China, a representative from the U.S. Embassy made a stop in our city, an event rare enough to make it worth trekking across town to have something notarized. We'd written a Letter of Application for Lily—just in case. At fifty bucks a pop, I wasn't exactly regretting we hadn't done anything more. Embossed and finished, it was the most emotionally-charged piece of paper I'd ever been around.

Some time after that, I was lying at the foot of Enoch's bed one night talking with him. After he fell asleep, I took advantage of the quiet and stayed in the dark to think and pray. Instead of straining forward into a future I couldn't see, I was inspired to look backwards. Maybe if I reviewed the emotional mileage I'd traveled over the past three years, I could unearth some comfort.

I started at the beginning. The joy of Lily Day. That match picture, our first sight of her. Just a baby. How excited we had been to show off that picture. Hundreds of people had seen it over the next months. I cringed over how oblivious we'd been to all that was coming. Then I thought about all we'd written, both public and private, while she was sick, and then the letters we'd received, and all the people who had prayed for her. I dwelt on the loss. Our grief. I dwelt on the years of silence while we'd raised Eden, and Lily became an orphan again, forgotten by everyone but us. Could we have prevented all this if we'd searched harder for her during that time? Finally, I mulled over the tumultuous months since we'd rediscovered her. My thoughts reached the present day. Still I lay there. Quietly, gently, into my mind came one thought:

I gave her to you so that you could know me better.

I only realized I was holding my breath when I let it out. The sentence, if indeed it was God who had put it there, had not brought joy. To be sure, the idea of the king of the universe wanting me to know him better was an awesome one. The deepest cry of my heart had been to know that God saw, that he was working, and that there was purpose and meaning for all we were going through. But this was decidedly not, "Hang in there, she will be yours in the end." God saying that would have sent me through the roof. This was different. It told me of the past, not of the future.

Another feeling was down there, niggling. Something familiar, something I'd felt recently. I struggled for the word as it hung back, just beyond pinning down, then, *oh. Right. Fear.* I was afraid. I was afraid of what the sentence seemed to imply. Namely, that growing closer to God might turn out to be the *only* reason he gave us Lily. I didn't know if "I gave her to you" meant the first time or both times. Depending on that, very different conclusions could be drawn. If it was "both," as I feared, then I knew the end of the story. And all we were daring to hope would be in vain.

God, I want to know you more. I am grateful and amazed that you love me enough to tell me you see. But will she finally be ours? Are you doing something here?

I waited a long time. I heard nothing more before leaving the room.

So that you could know me better.

Maybe through losing Lily, even again, God would accomplish things in me that getting her would not. Maybe he would redeem my pain in ways I couldn't see or dream about. But if the cost was losing her, I didn't particularly care to have those things. I'd have rather had her.

I didn't know what we would do if Lily became someone else's daughter. I couldn't picture what the death of hope would be like.

. . . .

We chose an upcoming holiday as a sort of self-imposed deadline by which we must surely hear some kind of news. But it came and went. It had been so long since we'd precipitated the hurry-up match, and we'd learned nothing since then. Would our first piece of news be that she was in America? Even that, we sometimes felt, would have been a welcome reprieve from the agonizing. Losing her two years earlier had been nothing compared to this. Then we had hoped, yes, but it was cut off quickly and we transitioned to grief. Now we hoped for the hopeless. Endlessly.

Days had multiplied to weeks and weeks had stretched to months as we strained to devise ways of coping with the unvarying routine of nothing happening. While everything happened. Inside us. We wrote, we talked, we cried. A lot of days we got sick.

Diarrhea is embarrassing. At least, that's how I grew up. Everyone gets diarrhea, but no one talks about it. You might tell your mom, or your spouse, but beyond that it's private; we frown on advertising diarrhea. I doubt my culture frowns any less upon writing about it in a book, but I've been liberated, you see. I've lived cross-culturally. I've seen that not every culture makes such a big deal about diarrhea. Not everywhere is diarrhea the forbidden topic.

"Where were you yesterday?"

"Oh, I had diarrhea. Thanks for asking. Did you all have a nice time?"

Interesting... you're welcome? "Uh, yes, we did."

Or, "Why is Mary absent today?"

"Oh, she has diarrhea."

And asked you to inform the class, I take it?

At first, conversations like these were about enough to make me feel like... well, I was raised not to talk about it. But the cross-cultural living won me over. When diarrhea's the issue, it's more convenient to mention it than to hide it. It's also a big plus going non-English and getting to escape our near-onomatopoeic version of the word, nausea-inducing all by itself. For instance, in Chinese you only get a case of, literally, "pull stomach." What is there to mind about talking of that? And, what with being unused to the water, unused to the food, and even, the locals really do insist, unused to the weather, it was a whole lot more convenient to be able to talk about "pull stomach" rather than hide "pull stomach."

Everybody got "pull stomach" sometime. There was no reason to be all hush-hush about it. You told others when you had a cold, you told them when you had diarrhea.

I had diarrhea all the time during our months of hoping for Lily. We both did. We were that anxious. Every day could literally be *the* day, the day we heard some kind of news. And our bodies broke down. It became so regular that we took to calling it *Lilarrhea*. But we didn't mention that to anyone else. We had our own customs to fall back on for some things; we hadn't dumped them completely.

Something else was purged from my system during those passing months: the word cruel. That theme from those initial days of wrestling had been a definite loose end I'd been unable to tie up immediately. But over time I'd slowly processed it, and by this time it had been eliminated from how I thought. I didn't yet know all that God was up to, but "cruel" wasn't where my struggles lived anymore. I wasn't worried I'd offended him by accusing him of it —I'd only been honest. He'd have known anyway what the seeds of my struggles were, regardless of whether I'd done the work of figuring out how to be totally honest with myself or not.

Through Lily, he had shown me so much about pain, about loss, about sadness. How many people were taken to those depths only by death? The death of their child, or of their spouse? He had been merciful to me. I determined to do my best to always remember, and never forget what it had felt like to lose Lily. Even if we were about to lose her again.

But I knew I still hoped.

I had to inquire again. I had to. I hated the thought of it— writing Rebecca—especially in light of my inquiry being ignored the last time. But we had to know what was happening. If nothing had transpired by now and the match was intact, it was as good as over; they were her family. Part of me wanted it over. Another part of me could have gone on waiting forever if it had meant there was still hope. Or that I wouldn't have to write Rebecca.

If there truly was no hope, it was better to bite the bullet, live through a little loss of face, and get it over with. Had God really said he didn't need my help? Or had he, in fact, said nothing at all?

At least my email got answered.

> Dear Dann:
> This darling child has a family that is coming soon to pick her

up. They are excited. The group home situation has been wonderful for Liu Hai Rou. I know that she will always have a spot in
your heart. She will be well.
Take care,
Rebecca Makos

So there it was. Final confirmation it would end.
We finally knew.

Moving Mountains

*We dare not make sweeping claims about the
promise of God's intimate presence unless we take
into account those times when God seems absent.*

Philip Yancey

ALL THOSE MONTHS, NOTHING.

We'd never stopped imagining the possibilities behind the
scenes. How she might come to us. But nothing. Nothing had been
happening. One little girl's adoption, which up until this time had
never proceeded normally, proceeded normally. No miracles were
waiting in the wings. Things stood now as things had stood at the
outset.

Nothing justified the hope we'd chosen.

We spoke together to clarify what exactly the news meant for
us, and I was surprised to hear that Tammy, too, concluded it
changed nothing. So even this news, remarkably, had failed to
vanquish our hope. If another family was going to come for her,
this was the expected time. If God was going to do a miracle, who
were we to say when all hope was lost? Who were we to give him
deadlines? I openly stated my willingness to give up hope if he told
me to, but otherwise, for me it was not going to be over until it was
over.

My hope would die when she left the country. Not before.

I left for Hong Kong on business. In our stage of life, the tab
for road trips was pretty much picked up by my wife. I got alone
time; she managed four kids by herself in a foreign country. I got
to read, think, enjoy peace and quiet, and journal; she wrangled

155

breakfast, lunch, homework, supper, and bedtime.

But on that trip there was a downside to my tranquility. Reality had all the space it needed to mock my foolishness. That there had never been any hope became so colossally obvious it made me sick. *Why did I ever agree to it? Why did I let myself hope?*

We didn't need the pain, and that other family didn't deserve the disrespect. It was a joke to think anything could happen at this late stage other than a normal finalization of not-Lily's adoption.

Thankfully, there is an antidote for foolishness: Put it down, get rid of it. So, for the first time since hope had chosen me six months earlier, I deliberated over how to kill it. If God was not working to bring about what we desired, I *wanted* it over. If the time for tears was past, I wanted them finished. If this was becoming somehow about me, if I was wallowing and reluctant to leave my pit, if I was dragging things out, then it was time to move on. I told God that if I had made an idol of my love for Lily, I wanted it taken from me. He had given me the love I had for her in the first place, and all he had to do was say the word. If he wasn't in the story anymore, I wanted to know. If he said "Drop it," I would. Or try to.

I put down my pen in one motion and picked up Psalms in the next. I began where I'd left off the day before, Psalm 126. I had to quit after three chapters, my mind bludgeoned by words. The day's reading might as well have been comprised of two sentences, still burning themselves into my soul:

> Children are God's best gift.
> Stand in awe of God's Yes.

> Permission to keep hope alive?
> A sign?
> I hadn't the foggiest.

. . . .

A few days after my return home, I turned around for a second trip, this time a Chengdu business conference. Two co-workers traveled with me. The coffee shop and culture center were growing, and I needed all the input I could get. A company run by an old friend of mine from Chongqing hosted the conference. The keynote speaker was a well-known American businessman, long-time China resident, and owner of a glass factory on the east coast.

And, as I was on the road again, I had a lot of spare thinking time. More and more I found myself admitting the adventure was over. All mystery had evaporated. Everything would soon end. Yet even now, a corner of my heart refused to bow to that logic; a remnant of hope festered there, growing fiercer.

In one of the last sessions of the conference, the speaker wrapped up with a story about a baby girl he and his wife had fostered for two years. That introduction jounced me from two days of productive business strategizing and abruptly returned me to Lily.

The girl in the speaker's story had come to live with them when she was only a few months old, and had displayed the all-too-common responses of the unattached. She'd been neglected and rejected for such a short time, yet could reject her new caregivers, emotionally and physically, like she'd been born to it. She needed so much, so desperately, yet couldn't receive. She fought the very comfort that could heal her. Pictures of the girl flashed on the screen, and my heart thumped, and my mind wandered away to a girl at that very moment transitioning from her Beijing foster home to her old orphanage to await her family.

The speaker was making his final point. He said that loving this girl had been an epiphany about God's love. Never before had he realized what the rejection of unconditionally offered love might feel like. He got emotional just talking about it, which triggered emotion in me. But I was completely taken off guard by his final words. He relayed what he had said to the girl as she pushed him away:

"I just...want...you! Lily! I...love...you."

It was the first time he'd mentioned her name. I nearly had to leave the room.

. . . .

I had one more appointment in Chengdu: a meal with friends from New Zealand who happened to be visiting someone else in Chengdu at the same time. They had followed along from the very beginning of our Lily stories, and had even been together with us when Lily's match had been taken from us.

157

During our meal together now, they surprised me with concern about Tammy. They wondered if in this second Lily loss she was suppressing too much of her emotion. The thought had never occurred to me. Tammy was being Tammy, and her responses were normal. She always kept a lot of emotion to herself. But I said I would mention their concern.

When I got home that weekend, Tammy didn't immediately resonate with their concern either. But, surprising both of us, the longer we talked about it, the more Tammy realized they were right. She had been keeping more emotion down than was healthy. She decided to open up.

The next morning she took an extended time to journal and cry.

> God, are You there? Of course: "I will never leave you." But right now—when my heart is confused and hurting, when I feel at a loss for words, when I need you most—I need to know You are here, that You hurt too, and that You understand deep pain that is impossible to explain to others.
>
> In other people's eyes, I should be glad that Lily has been matched with a family.
>
> Well, to tell the truth, it hurts. I feel so lost and confused. Why, why, why were we called to hope at every turn? To hope for something utterly impossible. Why did you allow others to have dreams about us and Lily? Why that movie of you doing the impossible right when I was begging to be able to give up hope and to be reasonable? Why the songs of hope and of you doing the impossible? Why the devotions and the studies of you moving mountains? What were You calling us to wait and hope for?
>
> Lily's matched family is coming to pick her up this week or next —then it truly is over. How do we deal with that? Am I that far from you that I have so misheard you? The many times I felt you were saying, "Hope"? The many times I felt you were asking me if I believed that You could do the impossible? Did You just want to know if I could believe, even if it didn't happen? I tried to believe, and now that the end is so near I want to continue to trust. Trust you with our hearts, trust you with our dreams, trust you with Lily.
>
> I know you know best. I want to trust your love. I need to know and to feel I can trust you, even (especially!) in dark times. But Lord, I do not understand what is going on. I feel weak and

confused, even angry at times, but I don't want to be a temper-
tantrum child. I really, truly do want your way more than what I
think is best. In all my venting I know you know that. And even
though the pain and tiredness is still here in my heart, I am going
to choose to trust You. Even though I cannot hear what You are
saying, I choose to keep seeking. In Your time You will speak—
and for now I will wait. I will wait, Lord. I wait for You.

Tammy emerged rawer and more vulnerable than she had been
since her Beijing trip, but thankful for the love and wisdom of
friends. I had gotten the kids ready for our usual Sunday afternoon
gathering with a handful of other foreign families. Neither of us
knew of the storm that awaited us there. Because of having just
opened herself, Tammy would feel the full brunt of its fury.

We headed out the door and were in our seats by the time the
singing started.

Then this lit up the screen:

> Savior, he can move the mountains
> My God is mighty to save, mighty to save.

It wasn't even the first time since Beijing. The song had followed her everywhere—each instance salt in her wound—and had
long since been irrevocably linked with her Lily pain.

Tammy fled.

God only knows what it felt like to have that song show up
minutes after making herself more vulnerable to feeling. So many
times she'd had to fight the lie that she did not know how to hear
God's voice. The lie that she was the problem. Now, once again,
just when she'd asked him if he would speak, she'd heard words
and was unable to believe they could possibly be his.

Seeing her walk from the room clued me in to what song I was
singing.

*Oh, God. That song couldn't have been sung last week? Or next? Why
today, just as she is so tender? God! Are you doing something? What are you
saying to her? Are you ever going to tell us what you are up to in all this?
Again this looks like an example of, just when we've asked, you not only being
decidedly not silent, but encouraging our hope. Will I look back someday and
recognize an overactive imagination? Have I been manipulating these experiences after asking you to speak? I haven't thought so, but I don't know what to
think any more.*

Maybe God was doing something. Maybe he had purposes for our hope, as illogical as it seemed, that lay outside giving us the object of our hope. Maybe he was behind the encouragement, allowing us to hope to the bitter end for reasons we couldn't see. Or maybe—hope really did refuse to quit in me—his great miracle was waiting to be gloriously revealed at the last possible moment.

Maybe he was willing for us to continue in deep pain because he knew it was leading us deeper into him. Whatever was going on, and no matter what end our road had, even the worst end, it was impossible to have so much agony and uncertainty and not long for something to redeem them. Pain is awful, but even the worst pain is nothing compared to the pain of pain proving ultimately meaningless.

Changed

君人求诸己，小人求诸人。

What the superior man seeks is in himself;
what the small man seeks is in others.

Confucius

STILL THE END TARRIED. Still we bled.

Tammy wrote to our email list asking them to pray. Lily was celebrating another birthday, and her family would soon be in-country to pick her up. She knew she could say something safe such as, "we are so happy she now has a forever family," but that wasn't what was in her heart. Her heart was hurting more than she could express, and way more than she wanted it to. She wrestled with questions that had no answers. Sure, there were polite answers lurking out there—"everything works for good, we will grow from this, this is for the best"—but her real world was her hurt. When we'd lost Lily two years earlier, Tammy had grieved that loss and moved on. This time—facing hope, meeting Lily, holding her, only to face losing her again—was more than she could bear.

"Goodbye, again" threatened to unravel her.

But what, Tammy asked God, could she do but trust? There was nothing else. We had to live with our doubt, our lack of understanding, and our limited perspective. But to lose trust in him would be to lose everything. She had no choice but to trust him with her pain. She had to cling to the truth that he loved her. She had to picture him hurting and crying next to her and with her. "I would be a spoiled child indeed," she wrote, "to only love and trust

Him when I get what I want, when I understand, when life is good. I don't want to love only because of what I see He does for me. I want to love because of who He is."

Tammy continued to press in to the wisdom of our Kiwi friends. She declared an end to burying her emotions in busyness. She ran to her one true Comforter. Together we began to share with each other more feelings. We were living the same difficulties, but we processed them so differently and had such differing emotions. We began to read each other's journaling more. And to pray together more. Love and support from others flooded Tammy's inbox as well in response to her newfound openness, and again those who had lost children of their own spoke most magnificently.

I bumped into Psalm 20:4-6:

> [May God] give you what your heart desires,
> Accomplish your plans.
> When you win, we plan to raise the roof
> and lead the parade with our banners.
> May all your wishes come true!
> That clinches it—help's coming, an answer's on the way,
> everything's going to work out.

Oddly enough, I didn't latch on to the hopeful language or take it as some kind of sign for us. I admitted it was over. I could affirm everything was going to work out, with the caveat that "working out" was going to look a whole lot different than what we'd originally hoped for. In spite of how great winning, parades, wishes coming true, and coming help sounded, I knew what the answer on the way could really be.

I was fully aware, however, that against all odds and any logic, a piece of me still hoped. It was unrealistic and ungrounded in fact or in anything we'd been told...but there it was. I pictured my hope like a rising balloon in a pine forest, going up through great boughs. There was no way it would last long.

The end had to come soon.

Psalm 20's first verse was a truly befitting read: "God answer you on the day you crash."

Our crash was coming.

I told God I was ready. "But we're gonna need you big," I journaled.

I couldn't have known how big. Or how soon.

Within the hour, we would find her online. We found her family.

We had searched the web so many times for Lily's Chinese name, I'd given up on it. After I'd put my journal down, I came out of our bedroom and saw on our computer an internet search of Tammy's from the night before. The results page had failed to load, however, so I reloaded it. That got my attention.

Liu Hai Rou.

There was a blog link, but I still didn't know if it was our Liu Hai Rou or something else. I clicked it. Never had slow internet been that slow, nor made my heart race that fast. The blog title appeared, and a single picture began to load one line at a time. Black hair. A child. Then eyes. Chinese. A girl? A nose. My heartbeat increased, I still couldn't tell. Finally a smile, lighting her whole face.

Lily.

Lily with a different name. Of course she would have. It still hurt. She would not be Enoch much longer, either. They were coming. Coming to take her home.

They were her family; we were not. For agonizing months we had nursed blind hope, all the while this blog existing. The archives showed it went back to the very beginning. I'd been writing to Lily on the train and her new dad had been writing here. Since *then* we could have known. In shock, I berated myself for not having searched more thoroughly. Why hadn't I searched more often, with different search engines, or within blog sites directly?

Regret laughed at me, malicious and whispering: *There were things you could have done differently. Should have done differently. Now everything is lost. You could have done something but you didn't. This family would have been happy to accept a different match if you had reached them immediately. Now it's too late. She's theirs. And why did you ever involve the agency in the first place? They were never going to be on your side. Why didn't you contact someone in Beijing directly? Your daughter could have come home. Lily could have been Lily, but she isn't. And she never will be.*

I stared at the smiling face on the screen in front of me.

She looked so much older already...

There was no way to prepare Tammy. I took hold of her hand, sat her down, then watched her read while it tore her apart. After a long time, she sobbed like I had not seen, nothing close, in twenty years of knowing her.

163

. . . .

What to do?

Free access to Lily's matched family, something we'd badly wanted in the beginning, was ours. We had wanted them to know about us when she was just a name and a face to them. We had said, and we were sincere, it was so we could give them their daughter's history. But in the backs of our minds we remembered how our friends had found the family who had been matched with their daughter, and the response they got. And we hoped. But the agency said no. They would not put us in touch with them.

Now we didn't need their permission. We had found the family ourselves. Here, thrown in my lap, was the opportunity to erase regret. If indeed I had failed to act before, now was my chance.

The power to say everything was in my grasp. That girl is ours.

But I couldn't. There was no truth in my regret. It was accusation. Lies. I had not failed to act; I had chosen to trust. I'd been as guilty of passivity over the course of my life as the next man, but not the past six months. At every turn I had prayed, I had hoped, I had asked, and I had waited. To say only now, with hope jumping ship, that we should have done this, or could have done that, would be to claim I was the sole cause of my own pain.

If I claimed to have been trusting God all along, only to berate myself for inaction once I was disappointed with the results, how could anything I would ever do be categorized as trust? The past was past. If I took matters into my own hands now, would I go so far as to actually declare intent to trust him no further?

I spent the next day with a dull ache that told me there must be tears down there somewhere. The blog made it perfectly clear that in their hearts she was their daughter, and who could have expected anything else? I could not fault them for that, clearly. At all. Still, it jolted me. And those tumultuous imaginings about what could still transpire to give her to us instead of to them continued.

Though none of those thoughts motivated my actions. In fact, I began to see access to them as a door to doing the right thing. For them. Strange beyond belief, I had a short email conversation with Lily's new family. We had some pictures and videos that I imagined no one else was likely to give them, and it was only right they should have them. So I sent them, not explaining why we had them. We didn't know what they knew about us. Maybe nothing.

I gained a measure of peace, almost joy, having done it.

They told me it meant more than I would ever know.

I didn't share all that was more than they would ever know. They did not need their upcoming union with their daughter marred by us. They needed our kindness. Respect. And distance.

They were coming for her in a week. We informed the kids at dinner. Haddie cried. I did not know what God was doing but told him I was going to trust anyway. I trusted him with my pain, praised him for what it had accomplished already, and admitted I might never, this side of heaven, understand the story I was living in. I told him to do his work, and I only cared if he got the glory. The journey was coming to its end. I would take the part I was given.

It was no small thing to begin our long goodbye to the road called Hope that we'd been walking on for so long. What would life look like after we'd taken the final step? I peered within, aching to predict my own future feelings, but I could not. The end was imminent, and still I did not know what I would feel.

A malaise covered everything.

Now that I knew we were losing her, what was important to me? Important to see? About myself? About all of it? I wanted something to stand on as I prepared for hope to be pulled out from under me.

I kicked myself for not thinking of it sooner: *Write her*. Like when I'd gone to see her and only knew my feelings after writing her a letter, that's what I needed to do now. Once again I could search for my heart by talking to her. Writing would dig the well that led to water.

I addressed her, not as Liu Hai Rou, or Lily, or Enoch, but by the name that would soon become the only one she knew.

Rachael,

You don't know me, but my name is Dann. A long time ago my wife Tammy and I were your matched adoptive parents. Since that time we have loved you. I have never come to fully understand the depth of love that God put into my heart for you these past three years. Time and again, words fail me.

But for the past months my life has been characterized by something additional—Hope. It sprang to life as I wrote you a goodbye letter on a train coming to meet you. And it has continued

on from that day to this. I realized that choosing to embrace
Hope at that time would lead to more and greater pain afterwards. It certainly has.

But if I had to choose again, I would Hope again.

I just learned who your matched family is—you will soon be
adopted by them. And that's how I know your name. As I assured you in that first letter, I now confirm: they love you.

As I needed to back then, I needed to today—I needed to write
you. And again like then, it's more for me than it is to you. I
write because somehow by doing so I locate where my heart is,
and see what I couldn't see before.

When I sat down to write you an hour ago, this is what came
out:

"I Hope"

I Hope, young Rachael, more than anything, that you grow up to
be the beautiful woman you were created to be.

I Hope for your health, your peace, your safety, your fulfillment,
your joy.

I Hope that God gives you the desires of your heart.

I Hope you know how much you are loved. I Hope your new
family's love for you becomes such a part of who you are that
you never even think about it, it just is.

I Hope that someday you know how much you were loved even
before they loved you. You were Created, dear one, and loved as
you were conceived. You were no accident. No human can tell
you why your life took the turns it did, but he knows. He saw. He
was watching over you. Watching you even as you were sick
those many, many months in your orphanage, on the brink of
death. But he spared you, and brought you to your beloved
foster family in Beijing. You didn't die. The love you experienced
there was an extension of his—how they prayed for you! Prayed
for you until you were well. Prayed for you until you began to
thrive. And worked with you and loved you until you caught up
and made up for so much that had been lost while you were sick.

I Hope I never forget the question he asked me on your half-
birthday, the day that we met and the only day that we had
together. He asked me if I thought it possible that he loved me
as much as I loved you.

I Hope I never forget my answer, "Wow! I guess I don't believe that you do…"

I Hope that you come to know "Jesus loves me" is not only meant to be sung. Nor merely believed. It's meant to be experienced.

I Hope I can learn to live from that place always.

I Hope especially to live from that place if ever again God's actions seem cruel to me. I wrote in my first letter that losing you a second time—especially because it was precipitated by our very inquiry about you—seemed cruel. I've journeyed through that and am no longer there. Believe it or not, I am even thankful for the pain of these past months. Because I have loved and lost you, and especially because of losing you this second time, he has changed me deeply. I would not exchange that for the pain if I could. Somehow, Loss has become Gift.

And I Hope that makes a difference in me for as long as I live.

I Hope that I never go back to having a dull, slow heart.

I Hope I never go back to empathy being an unknown emotion.

I Hope I will be able to cry with other people in their pain.

I don't know if we will ever meet again, Rachael. I spent many days of the past months hoping that he would do the miracle of giving you to us as our daughter. I cannot have that hope any more. But I know, as strong as Hope was at times, it was always only in alignment with what he would do, never in opposition to it. So even now, I can take comfort in knowing that he makes no mistakes. And so my own journey enters a new stage. I don't know where it's going. But I do trust him.

Finally, I Hope for nothing more strongly than for you to know you are first and foremost His Daughter, and of all who were ever "father" or "mother" to you, none compare to your One True Father whose love for you will never, ever fail or falter. And it's funny—writing this, as I predicted, has now made me realize that the question grown to loom the largest in my heart now is this: will you come to know this?

I Hope.

Once your Daddy, just for a little while,
Dann Johnson

I had my bearings again.

And peace. At least for the moment. As usual, just because I felt something one minute, in solitude, did not necessarily mean it carried over to how I felt the rest of the time. A weekend passed, and Monday found me journaling again about being back to emotional zero. Maybe it was because I knew she wasn't Lily any more. Maybe I was in shock. Or perhaps I was still, call me crazy, hoping. My inner void confused me, and I didn't know if it was me being me—incapable as always of predicting emotion—or if once the rash of activity stopped, everything would rush back in. Was it possible, on the other hand, that I had simply given her up? This quickly? That would seem a miracle, but then, if my love for her was from him, didn't it make sense he could ease it away?

"My heart feels dead, God. Nonliving. Like before. Since I am supposedly a thinker, not a feeler, do I just say, 'oh well'? What if I said I'd prefer feeling to not feeling? Have I really changed at all? Or did I just think so? Surely it's not just my thought processes that have changed, my heart untouched? I was banking on the fact that you'd changed me."

At least I recognized how much journaling could do for me. The more I wrote, the more clear it became that my greatest hopes had begun to be for her well-being. Even as our connection evaporated.

I told God that the last thing I wanted out of the entire Lily experience was to lose all I'd gained, forget all he'd said and done in bringing me closer to him. That would be the worst. How many times would I have to experience "Jesus loves me" until I knew it deep in my soul? When would it become such a deep part of my reality that I didn't question that he loved me specifically, rejoiced over me for me? That he desired me close?

We braced ourselves for the end of the road. We wanted the best for Lily. We wanted God, the Father to the fatherless, to watch over her. It did not look like she would be fatherless for long; we implored him to care for her just the same. One morning Psalm 31:9 summed me up remarkably: "Be kind to me, God—I'm in deep, deep trouble again. I've cried my eyes out; I feel hollow inside." Then verse 24: "Be brave. Be strong. Don't give up. Expect God to get here soon."

I did expect it. I had to have his presence. We had to. Without it, nothing was anything.

The death of hope for me had always been pinned to Lily's adoption finalizing. Repeatedly I had affirmed to myself and to Tammy, "For me, it will be over when it's over. When she goes back to the States, that's when it's over." Before then, I didn't even bother trying to stamp out the last vestiges of hope that dreamed stubbornly on about things that could still happen.

Tammy failed to stamp out hope as well, though she fought it harder than I did. It didn't help either of us when I stumbled on the blog of another adoptive family who had just returned home from China. They'd met their little girl and changed their minds. They never took her home. Of all times to read such a story. Tammy could not process it: "I dare not dream, I don't want to hope. I have already done that."

We knew within a day or two when their pickup day would be. A Monday or Tuesday. On the Sunday before that, someone hand-ed me a copy of Mary Beth Chapman's *Choosing to SEE*. I had heard of the tragic death of Maria Sue Chunxi Chapman, but I did not know the story. It had occurred during one of our preparation times for moving back to China, and I'd heard only the vaguest details.

I did not put the book down until I had read it through. And inside me, a piece of the dam broke.

> Oh God. Yesterday I read *Choosing to SEE*. There are no words. I'm almost a faucet this morning. I stayed up till 2:00 AM finish-ing, and after Eden came in for a morning snuggle four hours later, I couldn't go back to sleep. I lay there crying. Crying for Maria. It was like I missed her, the pain of that loss was so real to me. I cried for Mary Beth. God, thank you for the gift of that book to my soul. And yet I wished with all my heart it had never been written if it could have meant it did not happen.
>
> I am in flabbergasted unbelief that this is me writing. What a miracle that stone-hearted, untouchable Dann can even write such words. I guess you *have* changed me. Thank you, thank you, thank you. For the pain. Without it, I know feeling theirs would be impossible. And yet it hurts. I have never hurt more for Lily than I did for them while reading that book. The ripping, the tearing, the finality of death, the tragedy of their son, the empty, quiet house…God, I stand in amazement that I feel their pain. It hurts *so much*. How foolish and small I have been to live so many years knowing nothing of pain. Even of your pain. For us.
>
> I'm holding back on Lily, though. I feel it's coming and I know it's coming, but I think I'm waiting for it to be all over. Having tried and failed to rid myself of the corners of my heart still hoping for a miracle, I know for me that it cannot be over until it

is truly over. Then I can let myself go and finally grieve.

But do you know what? That is not today's step—even if they get her today we won't hear about it. So I won't ask for the faith to take it yet. I ask for the faith to take today's. One step, one day.

Give me yourself.

While reading Mary Beth's book, the readiest tears came every time she spoke of signs God was speaking to them. A friend's dream, a coloring page left behind by Maria, ladybugs. *God, you do love them, don't you? You are speaking to them, aren't you?* My tears were the welling of hope that he was speaking to us, too. Even if for most of our story there'd been silence. Even though some "signs" had finally shown themselves not to be, or at least not signs of what we hoped for. Therefore I devoured as well Mary Beth's passages about bewilderment, unsureness, and silence.

And signs continued to appear. Either that, or we were insane. But we could not put our faith in them like we could in him. Some things we just didn't know. Some things always remain mystery. We had never claimed he'd promised us Lily. We had only hoped.

The Ending

I closed my eyes and she slipped away.
She slipped away.

Boston, "More Than a Feeling"

THE ENDING WE'D YEARNED for was not the ending that came.

Lily's adoption had finalized, whichever of the two days it had been scheduled for. Hour by hour we imagined them flying with her to Guangzhou to complete the U.S. side of the process, seeing the same buildings and rooms at the consulate that we had with Eden. We speculated about what restaurants they might choose on the island that was home to the White Swan Hotel.

Liu Hai Rou was Rachael.

We had a work meeting. Tammy would have rather not gone, but she never could skip responsibility easily. Extraordinarily, a team member opened the meeting with a short devotional that included one of the verses from Song of Solomon that had sparked Lily's name choice.

Tammy's look made me wish I had a paper bag to give her, but she gripped her chair and held out for the singing, hoping that could distract her into keeping herself together. But it was not to be: song number two was the moving mountains chorus.

She lost control.

I'd never seen it happen. She never wept in front of other people. Most of our lives together, not even I had been privy to her tears. And though in the past days she had been giving herself broader permission to shed more of them, I knew total public collapse had never been part of the deal.

171

As her sobs got louder, I was as unsure what to do as anyone else. Thankfully, by a stroke of luck[41] I made the right call (she told me so later) by signaling madly for everyone to ignore her and continue on. We sang some more and she had the time and space she needed to compose herself. Later on, and she could by then appreciate it, everyone gathered around and prayed for her. For us, and for Lily. And for her new family.

That night Tammy sent a letter to all those who had followed along with us so faithfully from the beginning. Her final Lily update. She had come to see God's hand even in her breakdown that day. She hadn't wanted to let others in: it was hard enough for *her* to grasp the emotions she had for this girl she had spent one day with, how could anyone else understand? But now she saw that a large part of her refusal to cry had been fear of judgment. "Get over it, will you?" or "What is the big deal, move on already!" The collapse had made those worries moot and provided her with other —better, tougher—questions: Will I learn to hope again? Am I still capable of taking steps of faith? Will I be able to deal with life's future disappointments? Will I ever be able to trust that God moves mountains again?

Tammy believed God had asked her to ask him to move the mountains that stood in the way of us adopting Lily. Now she had to wonder: Did I hear him right? Did he want me to ask? The next time he leads me to ask, will I be able to believe it's him? Can I continue to risk taking steps of faith? The questions which surely flood the minds of all those who pray for miracles, or healing, or deliverance—but don't get them—flooded hers.

Tammy closed the letter to our friends with the story of a crippled mentally disabled boy and his grandmother that had turned her perspective on its axis that day. We had seen them on the street right after our work meeting and stopped to talk to them. The boy's body was bent and helpless, and in the eyes of many who walked past, he was hopeless, even worthless. But his face had captured her. She wrote that it had felt "like looking into the eyes of Jesus," and that she longed for her faith to mirror the simplicity she saw in this child's face. She closed her letter expressing "hope and trust in the One who loves me best."

A day later, she did not bowdlerize her personal journal:

Lord,
What do I say today? I guess I am feeling just plain angry. I even

felt angry that we ever knew Lily. My thoughts were, 'Good riddance! I don't want to think of her again. Hit the road, and don't come back!'

She came once and brought joy, then pain. She came again and only brought pain, pain, pain. Anger, confusion, lost-ness, pain, anger…and this is supposed to be good?

I can't hear You. I don't know how to hear You. I don't know how to feel. I just feel blank, dull, and angry.

I hate having all this anger and fighting in me. I feel so lost, so out of control, so powerless, and I have so many doubts right now! Is there any point in asking for help? What if everything I have believed in all my life is not real—what if there really is no hope? Oh God!

If I can't have You, I can't have life. My life, my dreams, everything is worthless. You really are all I have. I can't lose You, but I feel I am drifting. Like You are far off.

And as if the loss of hope isn't enough, now I am having problems with Dann. All I have gotten the last few days is the silent treatment. If ever there was a time I wanted to crawl under the covers and wish everything away, it's now. But that wouldn't make it go away—everything will be here tomorrow. And the day after.

Are You *there*?!

Or am I just talking to myself? How much of You is my imagination and how much is real? I don't doubt you exist; I fear I don't know You. That I can't know You. I doubt that You want to know me. After all, who am I? I feel like I just lost my best friend. Like when I need You most, You are gone, leaving us to just flail around.

I know others would tell me You are writing a story, etc.

Well, I don't *like* this part of the story!

Two friends who had lost children wrote the healing words that pulled Tammy back from the brink of despair. Her journal entry the next day was much more the type of writing one normally expects to make it into a book.

She still trusted.

I, too, knew I faced the systematic processing of the end of hope. I, too, would have to write. But I was torn as to how to begin: did I want to address my written thoughts to God, or to Rachael? The fact that I so quickly settled on the latter alerted me I must have some reason for hesitation with God. Why? I wrote him all the time about everything, why resist now? Was I angry?

It was possible. Moments earlier, walking to my office, I'd had a sudden violent urge to curse at a total stranger. There had to be more beneath the surface than was openly apparent to me. I decided to figure out what. I would write them both and see what came of it. Writing had always helped before.

The letter to Rachael started out cranky and got worse. From the start it uncovered anger. I was angry she was adopted, angry it wasn't us. Much worse, I discovered that I still hoped for something to happen that would bring her to us. The long-awaited and pre-appointed hour of death for Hope was past, yet, betraying me, it refused to die. I put the wacko scenarios running through my head down on paper, sure that if shared with anyone else they would generate an intervention. My words were the words of a man losing his grip.

I wanted to promise her we'd love her forever at the same time I wanted to be free from ever thinking of her again. I feared never being able to let go. But how could I do the opposite: say a mere goodbye and have it be over, just like that?

Because you have no other choice, idiot, that's how.

Maybe all her neglect-induced problems would make her a terror. They wouldn't know what to do with her and I would swoop in to save her a third time. Disrupted adoptions were rare, but they weren't unheard of. The thought that the adoption might not go well didn't horrify me; it comforted me.

My writing began to sound like nonsense. Even to me. I quit mid-paragraph, never concluding how I felt, not knowing what else to say.

I was numb.

It felt like the entire three-year ordeal had been for nothing. As if everything I'd gone through had in the end conspired to teach me nothing and change me not one iota.

I let Lily go.

And hoped for nothing.

> And so it's your turn. Ha, as if you were equals with her. I know you're not.
> Here goes.
> God.
> Man, you could have given her to us. I know it.

But you didn't.

You didn't want to. And of course I know I couldn't see the whole picture and of course I know you weren't being mean and of course I know your ways are higher and better and of course I even know this pain has accomplished a lot. Is there more pain to come? I don't feel any right now. I just feel like, "Whatever! Enough already! Let's stop talking about Lily 'cause there is no Lily!"

Why? Why the whole narrative? Was it really the only way to accomplish what you want? Dang, I can't even finish handwriting a question before I know the answer. And have moved on to harder questions.

This is the crappiest journal or letter I've ever written. I don't even have a clue what to write cause I feel like there's nothing in there. Forget it for now.

Even writing had deserted me.

But the next day I couldn't help but take it up again. This time to write a letter, as Tammy had, to the friends who had been with us from the start. One last snapshot of the heart as the final curtain dropped. Our journey through the valley that had been Lily had reached its end.

I informed everyone that Lily had naturalized as a U.S. citizen.

I thanked our friends for their encouragement and prayers, even those prayers asking God to put Lily in our family. Not getting the answer we wanted didn't mean we weren't glad for those who had stood with us to ask.

There was nothing else to say.

Or so much to say, I had no idea where to start.

Job, the one man in history who may have lost the most, has God finally address him: "Brace yourself like a man" for some questioning, Job. I knew all those questions God asked. I knew all their answers. I agreed with Job's conclusion:

> I know that you can do all things;
> No purpose of yours can be thwarted.
> You asked, "Who is this that obscures my plans without knowledge?"
> Surely I spoke of things I did not understand,
> Things too wonderful for me to know.[42]

175

But when he continued: "My ears had heard of you. But now my eyes have seen you," I knew Job was leaving me behind.

For I dwelt in between those two lines. I'd heard of God. My faith wasn't wavering. But I needed to see him. Again. Right then. In my pain.

Many of my talks with him were still originating from the place in my heart where I wished things could have been different. I knew I was wrong—things weren't going to be different—but it was anything but wrong to be real with myself. And with him.

I still wished for Lily.

But it wasn't going to be. Ever. Not her. Not us.

For some reason God had put overwhelming love in our hearts for one little girl without parents. Now she had them. They just weren't us. He was still God.

"Today," I wrote our friends, "Hope ends."

Those who wept with us were enough.

Valleys are first survived, not explained.

Yet, Hope

Heart-shattered lives ready for love don't
for a moment escape God's notice.

David, Psalm 51

IT WASN'T COMPLETELY OVER.

We still had to grieve.

Our former daughter's departure gave us permission to begin.

At least grief would put an end to the strain of hope. And experience told us we would survive. What I didn't expect was how hard I would have to fight to put down hope. Long after I'd assumed I'd be done with it, I still couldn't kill it. I still hoped for something to bring Lily to us. Again and again I was driven back to God to plead for help in putting an end to something that had gone past the point of all appropriateness. Only slowly did it fade.

And we grieved. Like three years earlier, only this time longer. In the throes of grief, it was difficult to catalogue all the ways the Lily valley had changed me, but very quickly one conclusion rose above all others with crystal clarity, though I could not believe it:

I had room in my heart for one more.

All along I had said the opposite. I'd wanted Lily, not adoption for adoption's sake again. Any preparation, any paperwork, in my mind had been for her alone. Our family was already big, by China standards huge, and I had no desires to add a fifth child. Furthermore, we no longer had the modest savings we'd had for the first adoption, we'd probably have to move to a bigger apartment, our salaries probably failed to qualify us for China adoption again anyway, completing a dossier from this side of the world sounded

177

like a royal pain in the neck, and the merest reminder of Eden's transition difficulties made my flesh crawl.

I was just getting warmed up. Reasons against adopting were bountiful. Those in favor seemed to be two: there were children in need, and we appeared willing to love one more of them.

How are those two reasons compelling? They're applicable to just about anyone.

But the final nail in the coffin of my resistance was impossible to fight against: God was the one saying this. He specifically wanted this for us. I didn't know how I knew, I just did. There'd been no earthquake, no wind, no fire, and no word, even whispered. It was still clear. I knew that I knew.

I half-grudgingly relayed as much to my wife, who then confessed she'd been secretly on board with the idea since my Psalms story from Hong Kong about "Children are God's best gift." She'd longed for Lily as much as I had, but way back then she'd known. If we didn't get Lily, we were meant to love another. Now she didn't need to be asked twice. Starting the paperwork right away would give us a good chance of bringing child number five home before another move back to the U.S. the following summer. Dossier-compiling commenced immediately.

I had a different matter of business to attend to. *OK, God. This was your idea. With all due respect, I would like to go on record as reiterating that it was not mine. I am sending you the bill.*

We applied for grants and raised funds like we had before. Some money came in, but less and more slowly than for the first adoption. Some close to us lovingly questioned to our faces the wisdom of our choice. Everyone had some idea of how difficult the road had been with Eden, not to mention Lily. My reply was standard: "It wasn't my idea."

It was still a thrill, come February, to get referral pictures of a precious daughter. She was almost three, and her reason for being on the special needs list was an easily manageable blood condition. We joyously began the match period, and to love again. We didn't hold back.

We had eight thousand dollars raised of the estimated thirty needed. But I wasn't worried. We never considered the money problem to be our own. This adoption had been his idea, the money was his problem.

Two months after the match, I was headed to bed on a Friday night. Tammy was already in bed, and I checked email before shutting down the computer.

> Dann and Tammy,
> I tried to call you in China, but couldn't make it work.
> From time to time, an anonymous donor in another state asks us to send them info about one or two families, and they decide how much they would like to contribute. We have been waiting for a response about you, so that's why your grant award has been delayed. Sorry.
> But the good news is that they have awarded your family $22,000!
> We are so thrilled.

I woke Tammy, not something I often dared do, to tell her the crazy news. After laughing and gawking at the email for a while, we tried to sleep, without success. One or the other of us kept giggling, which only got the other started again. With one stroke, using someone we didn't know and had never met, God had just covered the rest of our costs. Everything. Eight plus twenty-two equals thirty.

It would take us two days to pick our jaws up off the floor.

The school year in China wound down, and we prepared to move. Sadly, we had to return to the States without our new daughter, but it was only a matter of weeks before Tammy and I were turning around for a flight back to Guangzhou to get her. Our family went to seven.

Almost nothing about our second adoptive transition resembled Eden's. Our new little princess would have been sooner described comatose than a screamer. We didn't have her long before we suspected the blood condition might be the least of our worries. It was months before a personality started peeking through. Even years after adopting her we would still be measuring her progress in baby steps instead of the leaps and bounds Eden had taken. Our regular vocabulary expanded to include things like MRIs, brain cysts, 24-hour EEGs, anti-seizure medication, low muscle tone, midline dysfunction, and occupational therapy as we sought the diagnoses that would make sense of her continuing delays. One doctor told us she would never live independently. Another projected her mental development to peak at age ten or twelve.

But not once, no matter what has come, have I ever doubted

that this girl was meant to come to me, or that she belongs with us. Not for the tiniest fraction of a second.

I hoped for Lily as a daughter, yes. Desperately. But he gave us this one. I know it.

Nor do Tammy and I feel the least bit discouraged about our number five's future, whatever it might be. We hope to see much that is wrong now—neglect in the early years leaves deep scars— fall away as she attaches to us more deeply. We see love and work and persistence and prayer producing miracles of progress. But no matter what comes, we are completely at rest that she, and we, are in the hands of the One who dispels fear.

Her future is bright.

After all, there's her name. She was named for the journey that brought her to us. Her name is Hope.

Epilogue

All they knew was that they spoke of a glory yet to be revealed—a wondrous something yet to come, wherein their soul rejoiced, yet knew not why; and though it be not so in the physical, yet in moral science that which cannot be understood is not always profitless. For the soul awakes, a trembling stranger, between two dim eternities—the eternal past, the eternal future. The light shines only on a small space around her; therefore, she needs must yearn towards the unknown; and the voices and shadowy movings which come to her from out the cloudy pillar of inspiration have each one echoes and answers in her own expecting nature. Its mystic imageries are so many talismans and gems inscribed with unknown hieroglyphics: she folds them in her bosom, and expects to read them when she passes beyond the veil.

-Harriet Beecher Stowe

DURING OUR MATCH WITH Hope, it struck me that we had never tried to find out what happened to Ding Jing Feng. An online search led to a blog that her forever family had kept during their adoption process. They'd been united with her on the Mother's Day just after my Seattle passport trip. We'd been home when they came through Xi'an, just too preoccupied with Eden to have thought of trying to find them then. Our hearts melted to see the name they'd chosen for Ding Jing Feng: Hope.

The final blog entry date was over three years old, but I left a comment anyway. I told them we'd had a small connection to their daughter. I didn't know if they would see it, but not long afterwards the mood for a stroll down memory lane must have struck them, for they pulled up the blog and stumbled across my comment. After connecting and swapping stories over email, we made plans to meet up the next time our family was in Chicago[43] to visit my parents. Hope's family's church was at the end of the street where I'd grown up.

Meeting that family was like tasting heaven as we heard how God had woven together the story not only of their adoption, but of their lives. It was other-worldly to sing together in the worship service, laugh afterwards with a beautiful girl who was unrecognizable from the Ding Jing Feng pictures, and talk about all the girls: their Hope, our Hope, Eden, Lily. All four were interconnected. It left me speechless to see how Tammy's prayers for that little girl had been answered, and how we'd lived to see the grace that put our two families together.

. . . .

Again the end of a year in the U.S. approaches.

Hope has been with us the whole time.

After a long Northern winter, spring finally arrives.

Too long has the motorcycle I bought for this year sat in winter storage. A road trip is called for to make up for lost time.[44]

The bike licks up the miles and my mind wanders to Lily.

I make a stop one state over to visit old college buddies, then keep riding.

I cross a second state line before turning around. Once home I tell Lily about my trip in another letter.

The last one.

> Dear Lily,
>
> I know you've had another name for a couple of years now, but I still call you Lily. Today is your birthday. I hope it's fabulous.
>
> I took a long ride on my motorcycle last week. I prayed for you. I prayed for your parents. For your family.
>
> I prayed that your emotional connections with them would be deep, and that you would attach in all the ways you missed out on as a little one. And that in attaching to them you would grow up emotionally healthy. I prayed that all that was lost in those years without a family would in the end be fully restored. Redeemed.
>
> I prayed that you would be happy and healthy and know uncon-

182

ditional love. I prayed for freedom and victory and life, and that your whole family would know meaning and purpose and joy.

Then I was done. I turned around. It took two days to get home. I cried on the second day, but returning home was all the sweeter because of it. I hugged my five kids. Especially tightly did I hug Eden, the girl who is my daughter because you were sick. And Hope, the girl who is my daughter because you were lost. They became my daughters because you did not.

To celebrate me returning from my trip, we had Family Movie Night and watched the same movie we do every year on your birthday. I cried in the usual spots. One scene especially gets me, maybe because nobody speaks in it, and I, too, am silent. I write you letters but never give them. I pray for you, but you've never heard me. I love you, but you don't even know that we exist.

We have fully released you to be daughter in your family, Rachael. But you will never cease to hold the place of daughter in ours.

Because I loved you, Lily, and lost you, and especially because of hoping for and losing you the second time, I am not the same as I was. You have forever altered my life. God changed me using you. We will always love you, and what is best for you is for our love to remain secret, far away, and unknown. You need your family.

You have our love forever, little lady, even if you never need to know it.

We pray for you always.

Love,

You-know-who.

Or then again, you don't. I love you anyway.

It isn't Easter lilies or tiger lilies we think of in connection to our Lily. Those lilies are more typical lilies, at least in my mind, but they aren't her. She isn't a meadow lily, nor lily of the valley.

No, to us, Lily will always be *that* lily. The lily in our painting.

She'll always be a water lily. A lotus blossom.

Those are the lilies we notice. Those are the lilies we photograph.

Nor was a lotus blossom the lily I'd pictured when we named her. The verse in Song of Solomon 2 that we took her name from says "lilies of the valley" and I either pictured lily of the valley, the flower, or the "lilies of the field" in the book of Matthew.[45] Probably silly, I've fleetingly experienced regret a time or two, wondering if it wouldn't have been better to stick with a more common, immediately classifiable lily. To never have to worry about explaining to people that a lotus is a lily.

The first time I read The Message version of Song of Solomon 2, it about knocked me over: "I am…a lotus blossom from the valley pools."

Damn? A lotus is perfect, see?

It was always perfect.

Continuing,

> Look! Listen! There's my lover!
>> Do you see him coming?
> Vaulting the mountains,
>> leaping the hills.
> My lover is like a gazelle, graceful;
>> like a young stag, virile.
> Look at him there, on tiptoe at the gate,
>> all ears, all eyes—ready!
> My lover has arrived
>> and he's speaking to me!

To me.

He's speaking to you.

I might not yet know how much the-One-who-loves-me-more-than-I-really-know loves me. But I know it more than I did. And I will know it more yet. Someday we will know fully.

Come what may, conscious of it or not, he is here. Though valleys come.

Fear no evil.

Your valley widens.

Look. Up ahead, quiet pools.

And listen. Always listen.

Lily was my valley.

The very shadow of death.

And a lotus blossom. God only knows how.

Afterword

"KNOW YOUR AUDIENCE" MIGHT be the best communication advice anyone ever gave anybody. While I am not sure, China, how much of the surface I have scratched of your enigmas in my years living here, you were never far from my mind as I imagined those who might read our Lily story. I hope I never exhibited more concern for my own face than I had for yours. And before I ever wrote a word in English, I dreamed of the day it could be read in Mandarin. May it be so.

To the woman even now carrying that yet-unnamed girl or boy inside:
Never underestimate the value of that life. It was not only Lily who changed my life, but the woman who chose to give birth to her as well. That woman's time and our own time with that special baby have come and gone. We may still rejoice in the knowledge that a healthy girl lives on in her loving family.

To adoptees everywhere:
Only some of my children, never I, will understand what it is like to be you. You have a unique story. Could someone have loved you before you came to your forever family like we loved Lily?
Impossible?
But *someone* loved you.
First.
Best.
Loves you still.
Without earthly adoptions like yours, so many, many of the

rest of us would have missed out on so much. Your life is that tangible picture of heavenly adoption we could never have gained without you. Thank you. Countless people around you are privileged to love and be loved by you.

To my Mainland brothers and sisters:
The world yet has many Lilies.
Find her.
Find him, and love him.
Just one will do.
Love her with all your heart.
Not because she will be so blessed to have her life changed forever.

But because you will.

Dear Reader,

Thank you for choosing *Lily Was the Valley: Undone by Adoption*. If you're like me, you have more books to be read than you'll ever be able to get to, so I'm honored you read this one.

If you were blessed by *Lily Was the Valley*, I hope you'll share that. As I have never written a book before, I know almost nothing about the business of selling them. The only marketing team this book has is you. Your tweet, post, email, or other recommendation will do more to spread the word than I ever could on my own.

Perhaps one of the best things you could do for me would be to visit www.amazon.com/author/dannrobertjohnson. Whether your thoughts are positive, negative, or some of both, would you consider leaving your thoughtful and honest review of *Lily Was the Valley* there?

Thank you again for reading. And, should you decide to share with others, thanks for that, too.

Gratefully,
Dann Robert Johnson

Notes

[1] Commonly used in adoption circles, the concept of the red thread was traditionally used in reference to people destined to be lovers. This is a common translation: "An invisible red thread connects those destined to meet, regardless of time, place, or circumstances. The thread may stretch or tangle but will never break."

[2] "He's not exaggerating." -Tammy Johnson

[3] A phrase I borrow from Mr. Henry F. Potter's summation of Ernie the taxi driver's job in *It's a Wonderful Life*.

[4] Or one Edmund Hillary and one Tenzing Norgay, if one wants it more correctly and wordily put.

[5] Allowance should be made, I suppose (or perhaps this is only overly-optimistic author-speak) for the reader coming across this sentence fifty years from the date of its publishing. Nobody would have been waiting to adopt for *that* long.

[6] Though during some of our adoption experiences the China Center for Children's Welfare and Adoption (CCCWA) was still known as the China Center for Adoption Affairs (CCAA), for the sake of uniformity and clarity, "CCCWA" is used exclusively throughout.

[7] Among others, Song of Solomon 2:1-2

[8] "Ann spelt without an 'e' looks positively dreadful, whereas Anne with an 'e' is quite distinguished." Or at least so says Anne of Green Gables, whether in Lucy Maud Montgomery's book by that name, or as played by Megan Follows in the 1985 Kevin Sullivan production of the same. I doubt many named Ann (including some on our family tree) appreciate Anne's dogmatism on the matter, but then, it is an improvement on putting strychnine in the well.

[9] Years after her death, her children would pay for her name to

be engraved on an Ellis Island plaque commemorating her 1925 processing there, only to be subsequently informed by an older aunt that she had not passed through Ellis Island after all. It was an unnecessary stop for immigrants with official sponsors.

[10] Uncle Werner is the family member I most resemble. As a child, I could not have shaken the familial association had my life depended on it. Whether in my own country or the Old Country, every relative who saw me said the same thing: "Uff da, dat vun dere sartainly fayfers his Onkel Verner, dusen't he?" Even I myself once asked where a certain group picture had been taken, as I had no memory of it. My mom laughed and told me the person I thought was me was Uncle Werner in the 1940's.

[11] Okay, Tammy would almost certainly not have used the word "bode." Cut the author some slack, this is just a translation; this conversation wasn't in English.

[12] We knew Lily could be more dangerously ill even than we feared. It was the months-long duration of her illness that seemed to us most dangerous, especially as no doctors were making a diagnosis. We began to fear she might be in worse condition than anyone was being told. 1995's *The Dying Rooms*, although by that time in many ways a dated documentary and not representative of the situation in China at large, is nevertheless indicative of what we feared the most.

[13] In hospitals across China, patient care and meals are provided by relatives and friends, not by the nursing staff.

[14] This truly is a translation, not made until needed for this book. It would have been more difficult at the time to start with English and translate, for that would have meant starting with exactly what I wanted to say, then facing the impossible task of putting it into a language where I didn't possess the vocabulary. No, it had to be this way, starting with our feelings but only searching for Chinese that I possessed to communicate them as best I could. It took some effort to refrain from editing this translation, as I couldn't help wanting to make it read more like "me," but of course it shouldn't because the original doesn't.

[15] The Chinese way of referring to children. "Old big" and "Old two" and so on.

[16] My younger sister's letter is one:

If I could send my tears over the internet, there would be plenty to share with you. I am so glad to hear that they will still help Lily. Ever since I heard of her troubles, snatches of a storybook of her life have played in my head: how someone found her at the beginning, how she fought to stay healthy and even smiled on that couch there in the middle of her sickness, how she kept fighting for so long, how the angels assigned to her must have held her and helped her, how she might even know the face and touch of One who cared for her more than any other… And now to hear the rest of the story, that she will get help, and that without you she probably wouldn't have. Wow, the Author of that story is amazing. What a bittersweet role to play for you all. It just makes me cry. We're inspired by your words of courage and hope and love. What a thought that Lily was yours for four months and you have both changed each other's lives so deeply. The twins just turned four months, and they are so tightly entwined with our heartstrings I can't imagine how painful a separation would be. After Colin [3] prayed tonight, he said 'I'm the only one who remembered to pray for Lily!' Of course, then he gave himself away that he hadn't really been listening to anyone else. We all still pray for Lily every day. And for you.

[17] Words and music by Bob Benson and Phil Johnson, © Copyright 1975 by Justin Time Music (SEASAC)

[18] This particular part of our build-out circus exploded in a fiasco with our neighbors. The builder had originally passed code by cutting fire doors between all the building's units. Then, of course, before they could sell those units they had to seal up the openings. But in order for owners or tenants to subsequently also pass code, they needed doorways again, so had to cut them themselves. Which meant of course that everyone's fire door would always be locked from both sides, as no one wanted to expose themselves to theft. We cut a door into the vacancy on our north. When that space filled up, a screaming tenant showed up with the management office manager in tow, demanding I explain why I had cut a door into her space. Bewildered, and in one fell swoop shooting my cultural foot clean off while dooming my relationship with the management office forever, I pointed to the manager. 'Ask him. I don't want the door any more than you do.' The tenant said nothing else about the matter. Then, oh so shrewdly, while we were all home with our families on Christmas Day, she solved her own problem. We arrived the next morning to a view of a hastily lain and quickly drying brick wall behind our fire door. We had no choice but to cut a new opening to the south and hope the tenants who filled that space would be more agreeable. They were. But when they vacated a year later, burglars robbed our entire

center after breaking down that fire door. The management office claimed that the camera right outside only recorded to the opposite direction.

[19] Johnny and his paramedic partner Roy DeSoto, played by Randolf Mantooth and Kevin Tighe, respectively, can be enjoyed on the 1970's television series *Emergency!*

[20] Adoptees over a certain age do have the right to veto going home with a matched family after meeting them.

[21] Stories like this do not happen anymore. After the Hague Convention [http://adoption.state.gov/hague_convention/overview.php], all immigration paperwork is child-specific. Any rescinded matches today would require a family to return to a pre-child-specific point in the paperwork and begin again from there.

[22] Surely she must have said "line" like any American would. I guess living overseas has given me too many British friends to have not picked up an appreciation for *queue*. Though I needle them about what kind of word requires four superfluous letters which add nothing to the pronunciation of the one that was already there.

[23] The reader unfamiliar with Dr. Seuss' *Horton Hears a Who* would be well-served by taking a break to go and read it.

[24] The One Ring in J.R.R. Tolkien's *Lord of the Rings* trilogy.

[25] Although at the time of this writing, Terminal 3 is the sixth largest building and second largest airport terminal in the world, all three terminals of Beijing Capital Airport currently operate at or near their designed capacity. A new airport to the south is already under construction, the capacity of which will reportedly outstrip that of JFK, LaGuardia and Newark combined.

[26] For much of my life in China, Terminal 2 had *been* the Beijing airport, where numerous times we had picked up visiting parents come to see the grandkids. There is also a Terminal 1, but during our first years in China it was shut down for extensive renovations. Before Terminal 2's opening in 1999, Terminal 1 had been the entire airport. It in turn had, in 1980, taken over from the original terminal building. That 1958 building, which would have received Nixon's Air Force One in 1972, still stands, but is no longer used for any public flights.

[27] Show Hope, an orphan care movement founded by Steven Curtis and Mary Beth Chapman, gave us the grant. [www.showhope.org]

[28] Nothing she'd ever heard of drinking before living in Asia,

plain hot water is now Tammy's cold-weather beverage of choice.

²⁹ Before getting the chance to ask her myself, I wondered what Yao Shu Ting thought about the ceiling. Of course nobody really got her opinion. Asian gift-giving protocol can demand things of the younger, or lower-status person, even in basic hospitality situations, that my individualistic self fails to follow. Some gifts require nothing so effortlessly ascertainable as recipient preference.

³⁰ If I were a little older (LPs) or a lot younger (mp3s), "on" might be the correct preposition. But it's "in" because the only music devices around at that time were playing cassette tapes.

³¹ No China school teacher would have any concept of a summer break anything like this long, but we had three full months to do it in. When I myself had become a high school teacher, summer vacations were no longer quite so long, but we still joked that the three best things about teaching were 'June, July, and August.'

³² I learned this phrase from Dr. Karyn Purvis at an *Empowered to Connect* conference [http://empoweredtoconnect.org]. If you have adopted, are considering adopting, or want to better understand a family that has, we couldn't more highly recommend Dr. Purvis' book *The Connected Child*. Sadly, we did not find it until we'd adopted our second daughter. It would have helped us so much with Eden.

³³ Although modern usage of *condescend* has come to lean almost exclusively toward the negative side of connotation, I use it here as it was originally meant ("to descend to be with") and in the spirit of Jane Austen's Mr. Collins, rapturously basking in the condescension of Lady Catherine de Bourgh. In other words, in the best sense possible.

³⁴ This footnote could just as well have been inserted any number of other places. More than once in this book I have refrained absolutely from commenting on theological positions implied by some of my own journaling. They were written as journals, not position papers. I myself disagree with plenty of implications made by things I've written. The purpose for sharing personal journals is shining a light on my heart's processes, not declaring positions on issues. Attempting to adjust wording later to reflect personal change, maturation, disagreement, or even balance would be a disservice to the telling of the story as it happened at the time.

³⁵ How deep the Father's love for us
How vast beyond all measure
That He should give His only Son

To make a wretch His treasure
How great the pain of searing loss
The Father turns His face away
As wounds which mar the Chosen One
Bring many sons to glory
2) Behold the man upon a cross
My sin upon His shoulders
Ashamed, I hear my mocking voice
Call out among the scoffers
It was my sin that held Him there
Until it was accomplished
His dying breath has brought me life
I know that it is finished
3) I will not boast in anything
No gifts, no power, no wisdom
But I will boast in Jesus Christ
His death and resurrection
Why should I gain from His reward?
I cannot give an answer
But this I know with all my heart
His wounds have paid my ransom
Words by Stuart Townsend

© *Copyright 1995 Thankyou Music (PRS) (admin. worldwide by EMI CMG)*

[36] "Atropos"; Songwriters: Keith Daniel Hoerig, Andrew John Verdecchio, Michael Reese Roper, Dennis Bayne Culp; Published By: Thirsty Moon River Publishing Inc. 2008

[37] 'I have come that you may have life and have it to the full' — Jesus. How often has the mind-blowing greatness of this promise, to 'live well' (a desire spanning all cultures) been traded for lesser things (wealth, fame, pleasure) even though for centuries their impotence to meet human craving for real life has been repeatedly confirmed.

[38] No, not Treebeard. An ear, nose and throat doctor.

[39] I discovered that nose-blowing is even less socially acceptable in most Chinese situations than in my own culture. My sinus problems had become so serious there were times I simply had to blow my nose at the table, acceptable or not. On the flip side, I also made the bonus discovery that a good cleansing farmer's blow, one nostril at a time, onto the street is almost never a problem. As long as one's wife is not around.

[40] Some agencies do not allow families who get pregnant to continue an adoption process.

[41] 'Stroke of genius,' read early versions of the manuscript, though it was destined to evolve inevitably toward this final pinpoint of preciseness.

[42] Job 42:2-3

[43] We had driven there just for the weekend to attend an Empowered to Connect Conference (which we could not recommend more to adoptive families). Trust Based Relational Intervention® [http://child.tcu.edu/about-us/tbri/] was a lifesaver for us.

[44] For the reader who would enjoy visualizing my trip better with an accurate picture of the bike, the previous fall I had picked up a dark blue 1996 Kawasaki Vulcan 800 Classic with V&H straight pipes. A month after my trip I sold it for more than I paid for it.

[45] Matthew 6:28